SENT INTO THE WORLD

THE PROCEEDINGS OF THE FIFTH ASSEMBLY
OF THE LUTHERAN WORLD FEDERATION

EVIAN, FRANCE
JULY 14-24, 1970

Edited by LaVern K. Grosc

AUGSBURG PUBLISHING HOUSE
Minneapolis, Minnesota

SENT INTO THE WORLD

Copyright © 1971 by The Lutheran World Federation

Library of Congress Catalog Card No. 79-135216

International Standard Book No. 0-8066-1103-0

Manufactured in the United States of America

CONTENTS

Editor's Preface

Herewith the Proceedings of the Fifth Assembly of the Lutheran World Federation. It comes to you in a somewhat altered form from the reports of previous assemblies. As the contents indicate, we have included the major speeches and addresses, the Section Reports together with their resolutions and the actions taken upon them. The official minutes of the Assembly appear in an abridged form, listing, however, all of the actions taken and recording the resolutions and statements adopted by the Assembly. Lengthy discussions have been summarized, reference to all Assembly documents has been omitted. Personal statements are mentioned without reproducing the text, but a complete listing of all business items—73 in all—has remained intact. The complete and unabridged text of the minutes and specific Assembly documents are available upon request from the General Secretary, Lutheran World Federation, 150 route de Ferney, 1211 Geneva 20, Switzerland.

Although the official abridged minutes are printed here, it is obviously impossible to reproduce fully or include faithfully all aspects of such an Assembly. The Bible studies, worship life, list of delegates, innumerable personal conversations and confrontations, countless committee meetings, smooth-functioning technological, communication, and logistics apparatus are all assumed and presupposed.

With the goal of placing this volume in your hands as quickly as possible this volume has been prepared under considerable time pressure. It would not have been possible without the cooperation of Pastor Christian Krause, who bore the major responsibility for coordinating the corresponding German edition; Professor Eugene Skibbe, who did the preliminary editing of the Section Reports; and Miss Maureen Lee, whose extraordinary stenographic ability and industry were invaluable.

Geneva, August 14, 1970   LaVern K. Grosc

The Fifth Assembly 1970—Evian in Retrospect

Evian entered the annals of Lutheran history in an unexpected way. The road to Weimar, then to Pôrto Alegre, and finally to Evian, was long and strewn with obstacles. The work and the discussions prior to the Assembly constitute an important part of a unified whole, but ultimately this Fifth Assembly will be judged by the way in which the churches evaluate and implement the discussions, documents, and resolutions.

This introduction is meant simply to help the reader to understand the texts which follow by providing him with the backdrop against which to set the contents of those ten arduous working days.

The Evian Assembly differed in a number of ways from its predecessors. Never before had the churches of Asia and Africa played so active a role. Yet the beginning of the Assembly was marked not by harmony but by a difficult confrontation arising from a situation of conflict. It managed, however, to become an Assembly of dialog, a dialog broad enough to include groups which often find too little opportunity of making their voices heard in ordinary ecclesiastical assemblies. If Evian was characterized by the unexpected, this was due to factors and problems connected with the change of venue. This Fifth Assembly of the Lutheran World Federation was dominated to an unusual extent by a spirit of inquiry and desire for renewal.

I. Context

a) *Meeting Place*

On June 1, 1970, just six weeks before the Assembly opened, it was officially announced that we were still to meet in Pôrto Alegre. On June 5, a further official statement announced that the necessary conditions for meeting in Brazil were no longer assured and that the Officers had very regretfully decided to change the place of meeting. There had been no lack of criticism at the moment when the Federation was still adhering to its decision to meet in Brazil. The reversal of this decision brought an avalanche of protests and charges that the theme of the Assembly, "Sent into the World", had been betrayed. Then when it was announced that, because of its proximity to Geneva and its practical advantages, we were to fall back on Evian on the shores of Lake Geneva, the French resort was at once labelled "a city of refuge" and a "haven of false happiness"! Was the Lutheran World Federation seeking to evade the problems of the world into which it was sent, or was it merely concerned to prevent a breach in its ranks? This is not the place to go into detail. Suffice it to say that Evian was not a place of refuge or escape but one of genuine encounter. It was our purpose to take into account not only the situation of the host church but also of its specific context and even of its social, political, and human milieu. In the difficult and controversial situation in Brazil, this proved too much to expect. The shock caused by the about-face over the meeting place was too recent and the South American delegations too small to allow us to deal adequately with the Latin American factor. Our Evian discussions clearly showed how difficult it is for a world assembly to address itself to any specific situation. Whether we meet in a country whose government is challenged or discuss a critical situation from a distance, conflict is inevitably produced between those directly affected by the specific situation and those who judge it from outside. Some feel impelled to press for a public condemnation of the incriminated government while others can only fall back on a threat to withdraw or suspend their contributions to a body which cannot survive without them! This conflict threatens to paralyze the witness of any ecumenical organization. Its resolution depends on our attitude to the political responsibility of our Federation and whether we attach more importance to our national loyalties than to our Christian freedom.

b) *Composition of the Assembly*

Much has been made of the fact that, for the first time in the history of the Lutheran World Federation, young people (from 18 to 25 years of age) were full voting delegates. Previously, most of those taking part in these assemblies were representatives of the official church, their committees, and commissions, with a few parish pastors and laity, and a tiny minority of women. The official invitation to the Fifth Assembly stressed the need to insure a much broader representation of the whole church. The Executive Committee authorized each member church to send a minimum of two delegates, one of whom should be a layman.

Moreover the study of current problems made it necessary to invite a large number of consultants and specialists. In fact, not even half of the participants were delegates. This composition gave the Assembly quite a new character and made possible a dialog which at the beginning centered mainly on the youth delegates. Obviously, this Assembly was not dominated by the theologians; they took an important part in the discussions and were challenged by the very diverse representatives of the churches.

c) *The Spiritual Tone of the Assembly*

This is not easy to describe. At the beginning it reflected the critical situation in which the Lutheran World Federation found itself. But Evian will go down in the annals of the Federation as, above all, a "working Assembly". This description was already being used prior to the Assembly to stress the need to concentrate on the situation of conflict to which the church has to address itself both within and without. To some of those who watched us at work we gave the impression of being a very serious Assembly. They asked how we could possibly have consumed so many papers and produced so many documents!

For all of us the opening service will remain an unforgettable memory. Feelings were still running high as people arrived, and many were determined to make their strong criticisms heard. In fact this service opened in an atmosphere of disquiet. Thanks to a brotherly gesture on the part of the Catholic parish which allowed us to meet in its church, the service took place in an encouragingly ecumenical setting, in the presence of Cardinal Willebrands and the Bishop of Annecy. Yet the pain of seeing them unable, in their own church, to partake of the communion celebrated by their Lutheran brethren ruled out any false optimism and reminded us of the humility needed in tackling the problem of unity today. The opening hymns and prayers brought out the deep bond of unity between us despite our differences. The preacher chosen for this occasion made good use of the opportunity, exhorting us with the authority and freedom which are the privileges of the children of God. It is impossible to exaggerate the importance of this opening service, which through the grace of the Holy Spirit, set the tone for the Assembly, or to say how greatly we were helped by the excellent Bible studies each morning to recenter our discussions on the essential spiritual foundations.

Some have criticized the Assembly for restricting itself to pragmatic discussions issuing in resolutions which for all their variety and detail are lacking in inspirational power. Admittedly, we were much preoccupied with concrete problems and disinclined to generalities, discovering nevertheless real tensions among us. Some believe that the Christian community can only tackle its mission in the world on the basis of a profound spiritual renewal, a thoroughgoing theological stocktaking. They see this mission as primarily embodied in the witness of the individual Christian who grows more faithful in his discipleship through communion with God. Others, however, see a danger in this emphasis, which in the past has prevented the church from seeing its corporate responsibilities clearly and produced a dangerous dichotomy in its life. These call for a more complete involvement on the church's part, one which takes in the political sphere, demonstrating our ordinary humanity and prophetic forms of the love which God has shown in Jesus Christ.

Some observers thought that the Lutherans at Evian did not live up to their reputation, unduly restricting the theological discussions to which they are accustomed. It must frankly be admitted that we only skirted these questions and that they will have to be taken up again in discussions at the local, national, and regional levels in the coming months. On the other hand, it must be noted that Evian marked a new stage in the history of the Lutheran churches. They were no longer willing to consider theological and doctrinal problems in isolation but in direct relation to their implications for the church's mission in the world.

II. The Work of the Assembly

The pattern of the work at Evian was not altogether satisfactory and during the early days many spoke of their "frustration". Obviously a conference of 600 people is too large and unwieldy, especially since many of the participants were strangers to each other, coming from widely divergent backgrounds and thus experiencing language and communication difficulties. There is also the fact that there is no uniform procedure for such assemblies. Continental Europeans feel constricted by Anglo-Saxon rules of debate. Young people without experience of such ecumenical meetings regard Rules of Procedures merely as an aid to the Federation's Officers in controlling and manipulating debate. Discussion sometimes ran into difficulty when symbols and acts used by the young people were not understood by the rest of the Assembly! A future assembly should employ a quite different style, working primarily in small groups and avoiding the considerable waste of precious time in efforts to draft resolutions or reports attempting to register a general consensus.

The Fifth Assembly can be seen as starting from three centers of interest: the general theme, "Sent into the World", introduced by two major addresses, one by President Schiotz, the other by Professor Tödt. These two addresses did not influence the work of the sections to the extent we had hoped, mainly because at that stage the delegates were far more concerned to discuss the problems raised by the decision not to meet in Brazil.

The work of the sections added little that was new to the ecumenical discussion. It was content to rest on it and largely to identify itself with it. Section I showed clearly that proclamation and involvement are the concerns of the whole church and not just of societies and specialized agencies. The church is mission or it is not the church. Section II opened up new perspectives for the ecumenical outlook of the Federation. With respect to the church's responsibility in society a number of points seem to be established, despite differences of view expressed in Section III.

The Assembly experimented for the first time with "Open Hearings". Participants were able to focus on three aspects of the Federation's work, to learn more about these before deciding about future priorities. They indicated great interest in the work of the Federation and were very useful.

III. Provisional Assessment and Questions

The purpose here is simply to underline some of the main emphases of the Fifth Assembly and to indicate some of the questions left unanswered, which will now have to be taken up afresh.

a) Some asked as they came to Evian what future there was for the Lutheran World Federation and whether it could possibly survive this crisis. In spite of it, the Assembly demonstrated a profound unity, going much deeper than the differences and diversity of its members. There was a general awareness of the complexity of the problems facing us and a desire to work them out together. At previous assemblies, it had been the theological diversity which was most in evidence. What we saw in Evian was more a dialog between various kinds of church representatives: official delegates of established churches, experts and specialists, young people, the laity and so on. This diversity raised the question: who really represents the church? How can we translate the diversity of the church's constituency into structural and organizational terms? Obviously this problem is not solved merely by electing a youth representative and a woman to the Executive Committee. How can we broaden the decision-making process in the churches? How can we ensure that this diversity of groups actually shares in shaping the policy and strategy of a church? Here are young people who have shared in decisions affecting the future of the Lutheran World Federation. When they return home, since they do not belong to any executive bodies, they will find themselves more or less excluded from the practical implementation of these decisions and have very little influence with their churches. This applies equally to other participants in the Assembly.

b) The discussion about Pôrto Alegre clearly was more than a question of meeting place. It was also a question of the church's political role and the extent to which it should and could identify itself with those who suffer. It is in this context that the document dealing with the many violations of human rights, which constitutes one of the most important results of this Fifth Assembly, should be seen. It deals with the church's fundamental responsibility in this field and, of course, could not ignore the concrete situation in Brazil. Before we can define the Federation's role in this area, we must rethink the problem at the level of our different national situations. Whether we are dealing with individual liberties, racial tensions, religious persecutions, or economic exploitation, in each case we discover how difficult it is to reconcile different viewpoints based on biased information or on propaganda. Evian showed that Lutheranism is ready to assume its responsibilities in the contemporary world. One of the most important problems remaining unsolved is that of national identity and sensitivity and its relation to the catholicity of the church. This problem is perhaps even more urgent than the so-called doctrine of the "two kingdoms."

c) The already existing unity among Lutheran churches found expression in a resolution concerning full intercommunion between them. But what does this unity mean in terms of a common involvement in the world? Some hinted that the Fifth Assembly would be the last of its kind. It is indeed probable that its constitutional role could be carried out in a much simpler way. On the one hand, the Assembly is autonomous and makes the decisions necessary for the work of the Federation. On the other hand, the autonomy of the member churches remains unimpaired. What then is the status of decisions made by an Assembly, particularly of those decisions which affect directly the country or the life of a member church? Is this interference in the internal affairs of a member church? We certainly need to define precisely what membership in a worldwide communion means and what form the manifestation of the church at the universal level can take. In view of the diversity of our member churches, it is out of the question to make general consensus the objective of our research. Such an attempt would involve blurring distinctions and compromising the authenticity of our witness. Parliamentary democracy is, of course, essential at an Assembly but perhaps we need to make more room for minority views if we are to discover where the true consensus lies. Moreover, Evian demonstrated that this consensus was assumed to exist and that it was because of this that it was possible for us to differ and to oppose one another.

d) The Fifth Assembly dealt with ecumenical problems in terms of concrete commitment. The young people showed no aggressiveness in this area which some interpreted to mean that they did not feel on the defensive here. The contribution of the ecumenical observers and consultants was greatly appreciated. The presence of Cardinal Willebrands and the content of his address constituted a historic step in our relations with Roman Catholicism. As for the statement on relations with the Reformed churches, this opens up new opportunities for closer cooperation. Ecumenical discussions with the Methodists, the Baptists, and the Pentecostalists were added to those already undertaken with Anglicanism and Orthodoxy. We must also stress the importance of the statement of the Federation's attitude to Lutheran churches involved in union negotiations. In fact, disagreements in the ecumenical field were few. Here as well, we had too little time to consider the specific role of the Federation within the ecumenical movement.

Conclusion

The Fifth Assembly constitutes only a single element in a much larger pattern. It is imperative that we should continue the work which has been begun and tackle the many problems left unresolved. The Assembly clearly expects this work to be done not just at the level of the executive and specialized bodies but by a much wider range of groups at the local, national, and regional levels. In fact, the Assembly's work must continue at the widest level and this more effectively than perhaps was the case in its preparatory period, especially since we have learned that an Assembly is neither a beginning nor an end but rather a meeting point and a laboratory, and at most no more than a provisional statement. This Fifth Assembly has provided our churches with new possibilities. Certain things appear now to be firmly established: the fundamental missionary character of the church; the institutional and extrainstitutional limitations of the church; corporate socio-political action as a vital part of the church's witness. Under the leadership of its new Executive Committee and its President Mikko Juva, of its Commissions, Departments, and other organs, the Lutheran World Federation will continue to be available to help the member churches in broadening the discussion and hopes that they will derive great benefit from this wider debate. This volume is one such effort. If in the course of studying these pages, either individually or corporately, you have comments, questions, or criticisms, please forward them to the LWF in Geneva.

ANDRE APPEL
General Secretary, LWF

Geneva, August 1, 1970

MARC LIENHARD

Sermon at the Opening Communion Service
of the Fifth Assembly

Text: Revelation 21:1-6

Then I saw a new heaven and a new earth; for the first heaven and the first earth had passed away, and the sea was no more. And I saw the holy city, new Jerusalem, coming down out of heaven from God, prepared as a bride adorned for her husband; and I heard a great voice from the throne saying, "Behold, the dwelling of God is with men. He will dwell with them, and they shall be his people, and God himself will be with them; he will wipe away every tear from their eyes, and death shall be no more, neither shall there be mourning nor crying nor pain any more, for the former things have passed away."

And he who sat upon the throne said, "Behold, I make all things new." Also he said, "Write this, for these words are trustworthy and true." And he said to me, "It is done! I am the Alpha and the Omega, the beginning and the end. To the thirsty I will give water without price from the fountain of the water of life."

Lake Geneva may be calm, but the world is in unrest. This meeting beginning today may also be full of unrest, not least of all because it has not survived its birthpains. We will not, with a sweep of the hand, be able to wipe away "crying or pain" (Rev. 21:4), we dare not, because the suffering brethren should really be seen and heard.

There are our fellow believers in Brazil who have been deeply shaken by the change of Assembly site from Pôrto Alegre to Evian. They believe that they have been forsaken and their country has been falsely accused. But there are also others whose suffering, crying, and pain from this same country can be heard. Can we now calmly relax here at the lake and not hear all of this?

We cannot begin these days without confessing that we have failed these last weeks and months. We have failed in our serious intent to provide information. We have idealized our sentness and the romanticism of the Third World, or we thought that we could hold our Assembly in a strictly inner-Lutheran or apolitical setting. We have failed in our objectivity and our brotherliness, in our speaking and writing, and in our decisions.

We should not now be in search of fig leaves to cover naked human failure. We should not go hunting for scapegoats, but have the courage not to pass the buck.

Dr. Marc Lienhard, a pastor of the Church of the Augsburg Confession of Alsace and Lorraine, is a Research Assistant at the Institute for Ecumenical Research, Strasbourg, France. This sermon was preached at the opening service of the Fifth Assembly of the Lutheran World Federation which was held in the Notre Dame de Grâce, the local Roman Catholic parish church in Evian, July 14, 1970.

Nothing is easier to confess than the sins of others, but nothing is more important for a life together than conversation, confession, and forgiveness.

I do not want to say this in such a way as to cover with moralisms, but rather to speak of it in the dimension of the new heaven and the new earth, as we meet it here in Revelation. We know that the world which is seen here has already broken in upon us, on this earth. The vision of the seer is not, after all, simply the pious wish of a believer, or the apocalyptic product of a martyr who trades earthly misery for heavenly glory. The seer has really seen the coming world of God through the one who has come, Jesus Christ. How could he thus speak of the new Jerusalem, of the dwelling of God with men, of the overcoming of "death, crying, and pain", if someone in the third decade of the first century of our era had not turned things upside down? Were not, with this man Jesus, the lowly lifted up, and the established judgments surprisingly revised? Did not through him the barriers fall between Jews and Greeks, pious and godless? Neither temple nor sabbath, neither Pilate nor Herod, neither sacrifice to idols nor circumcision are any longer written with capital letters, even though they have not yet been written off. They no longer dominate the congregation of Jesus Christ.

If this service this morning has any meaning, then it is to take us into the reality of this new world, and, in the bread and wine of the altar, in the fellowship of brethren, and with the spoken word to place us in the dimension of the new heaven and the new earth.

Should we not herewith be permitted to shake old earth from our shoes? Should we then dwell on the questions which made the one who was born blind bitter— "who has sinned, this one or his parents?" Should we not dare to say: the sea, that is the guilt, is no more?

In the dimension of the new heaven and the new earth we not only become free from guilt but also from our selves, from the endless cycle of our own problems, and our little kitchens where the cooking is not always that good.

The vision of the seer is after all not concerned only with the church. It is concerned with it, but not with the church looking at or justifying itself, but with the bride adorned by God, which means the church that lives from forgiveness, from God's dealing with her, from the promise, and from the call. But even this beaming bride, in which the warty old woman, our churches, can hardly be recognized, is not at the heart of this vision. The heart is rather the dwelling of God among reconciled and united peoples, the new heaven and the new earth, and the overcoming of death, mourning, crying, and pain. This certainly applies to all mankind.

We in these days are called to see our world with the eyes and faith of the seer and to try here on earth to create something of the new heaven and the new earth.

This vision does not permit us to withdraw into the life beyond, for it was on this earth that Christ arose and is the "first fruits of those who sleep" (1 Cor. 15:20). Here and now we are to see and to build the new world on the already established foundation, and in anticipation of that which will be fully accomplished when "God will be all in all" (1 Cor. 15:28).

That means, after all, that in the cry of the hungry in Recife and Biafra, in the midst of the contesting students in Paris, and the self-idolizing nations, institutions, and world views, the world of the risen one is to take shape. This is true insofar as the risen one is the crucified one, who is on the side of those suffering and persecuted, and is eternally identified with the world of death, anguish, and tears. We are to live in this world and not on a pious and seemingly unpolitical island, and we are to be his instruments to build bridges—between east and west, between the 20% who have everything in bread and technology and the other 80%.

Down here, we as his instruments are to step forward against the beast of the underworld, the whores of Babylon, who have taken the place of God and allowed themselves to be worshipped as God, e.g., the totalitarian state, which on its own decides about good and evil, life and death; the revolution which claims that war is the holiest of instruments; against the consumer society which has exchanged the penultimate with the ultimate; the self-glorifying church which so quickly identifies its own decisions with the will of God.

Here below we are to open closed societies, to bring movement into rigid fronts, to allow the cry of anguish to become dialog, to create unrest, where man has buried himself in calm, and allow creative phantasy to rule, where boredom and senselessness have become partners.

This vision of the seer could broaden our little horizon in these days. Here there is more than alleviated individual misery, more than biblically legitimatized church politics, more than UN resolutions and world structures.

Certainly in the process we will also find the individual whose thirst can be quenched from the living fount of waters. It will continue to be the task of the church to be there for the individual in the midst of growing depersonalization and to proclaim to him that he isn't just a number or a thing, but a child of God. But how could we fulfill this task without bringing him into the fellowship of the reconciled congregation, and without trying to reshape the world in which he lives? Can we content ourselves with comforting consciences when Christ healed the sick, instituted the Sacraments, established fellowship, rose bodily from the dead, and shattered all religious and worldly orders?

If the future which is seen in the vision includes a new heaven and a new earth made up of nations gathered and reconciled around the dwelling place of God, then we dare not leave the matter of peace in the world to the professional politicians. Then I, as a Frenchman, must be uneasy today when extreme leftists are put in prison only to assure that the citizens may have a peaceful summer, and when the munitions trade is flourishing as never before, when conventions on human rights are not signed or sometimes ignored, even though on this national holiday one likes to say: *liberté, egalité, fraternité*. Then also here in Evian we dare not forget the tortured in Brazil any more than those who suffer behind other iron curtains.

The dwelling of God among men belongs to this envisaged future, which is already to take shape here. This is the real heart of the matter. And truly, we cannot just accomodate ourselves to his apparent "housing problem" here on earth. We cannot create a new world without a center, yes, this center. It is true that we have to change this world with as much energy as nonchristians, but we are to live and work as windows through which the mystery of the coming Lord may be seen. We are not to place ourselves self-assuredly as church or persons in the center, but rather are to live in such a way that, with or without words, it becomes clear: another stands at the center, another gives meaning to everything, another is the foundation. We are the children, but not the father. We are witnesses to the mystery, not the mystery itself.

We are going to "talk our heads off" about being sent, but will we allow ourselves to be sent? Would all that much sending into the world have taken place if we had flown to Brazil? We will never know, because it never came to that. But we have to face the sober fact that being sent is far more than a brief visit. Being sent in the dimension of the new world of God means real solidarity with and also the changing of situations.

By all means in Evian we ought to think through the question: are we prepared to let ourselves be sent? If we are only here for a rest, to speak noncommittally about the new world, without being willing to begin living it together, for each other, and for the world, then we can experience shipwreck also here on Lake Geneva. Then no wolves from Brazil or the press or from anywhere need to appear. We will then die on our own. Instead of living and working with a vision of a new world we will only be playacting, a churchly puppet show, with only the will for self-preservation pulling the strings.

We are called to be on the way. We can stand still or can follow it. We can stand still and do that which the church has done so often in the past, namely to offer static world views and laws, and confirm orders which are to remain eternally. We can also traverse the path for peace and justice among the nations, not equipped with ready recipes, but with the knowledge of the risen one, not armed with an ideology, but with a vision, which the world may see again and again through the risen Christ, a vision which with him changes the world.

18

On this path the church, by its own strength, can never escape the provisional and ambiguous. We have drastically experienced that in these last weeks, when the same motives have been offered for or against Pôrto Alegre. Complete clarity and final victory are not at our disposal in history. We are to humanize the world increasingly. In doing that we will not progressively climb into heaven, where all tears are wiped away and suffering, pain, and crying will be no more. That is really not in our control. Because of Easter we are able to joyously proclaim that God's last word is peace and not crying. That means that we do not just fold our hands, but we are joyously underway, always permitting ourselves to be blessed and sent by him, who alone can say: "Behold, I make all things new."

FREDRIK A. SCHIOTZ

Opening Address

In the name of our Lord, welcome to this Fifth Assembly of the Lutheran World Federation.

An introductory Statement

We are in Evian in France, but the blue print for the Fifth Assembly did not call for this. We were to have met in Weimar in Thuringia in Eastern Germany. At the time some critized this arrangement, but the Executive Committee did not waver and staff pressed forward with preparations. Then suddenly the DDR government withdrew its approval.

Into this breach stepped the Evangelical Church of Lutheran Confession in Brazil with a warm and a friendly invitation. Before the Executive Committee accepted the invitation, it assured itself that all delegates, irrespective of the country from which they came, would be admitted to Brazil. A further privilege was required; namely that the Assembly be permitted to function as a free Assembly. This assurance was provided.

The church in Brazil mobilized its congregations and people to provide what they hoped would be a memorable experience in hospitality. Preparatory work had continued over a span of three years. Two years ago questions began to appear about the military government that came into power in 1964. There were reports of repression and torture. In the summer of 1968 the Executive Committee reviewed the question whether we should continue with plans to meet in Brazil. They authorized the officers to make the final decision when they would meet in June, 1969. The officers decided in favor of continuing with plans to meet at Pôrto Alegre. But in December 1969, the Executive Committee once again reviewed the decision. After a day and a half of discussion, again the earlier decisions were reaffirmed.

During the winter and spring of 1970 new information of torture and repression flooded the public and religious press—first in Europe, then in North America.

It is clear that some of the information was wrong. However, it is equally clear that considerable brutality has been exercised by secret police. On the other hand there is no denying that the present government has arrested inflation, has succeeded in collecting taxes, and is using the money in worthy public projects.

When the officers met May 19-21, 1970, they were confronted with a rising wave of protest against the meeting in Brazil. The information that the Brazilian church wanted to make the Assembly a ceremonial event with President Medici bringing a greeting to the delegates was strongly questioned. Our host church was advised that the Assembly was to be a non-ceremonial working congress with greetings from government limited to local personnel. With this understanding the officers were willing to risk some defection among delegates and to continue with the plan to meet in Brazil. As late as May 31, your President instructed the General Secretary to proceed without hesitation with the arrangements to meet in Pôrto Alegre.

June 4, the General Secretary telephoned the information that the church in Brazil insisted on inviting President Medici to greet the Assembly. On the basis of information gathered by the staff it became evident that this insistence would bring large defections in delegate participation. What was the right decision in such a situation? Should we meet in Brazil with a sizeable contingent of delegates from large member churches absent? Should the Assembly be cancelled? Or should it be relocated? Your officers made the painful choice to relocate. Some have intimated that the decision was unconstitutional. In your President's judgment the situation your officers faced required the decision that was made. In his judgment it was not unconstitutional and he is ready to accept full responsibility for what was done.

What has happened raises a very serious theological question. We were scheduled to meet in Brazil at the invitation of a member church. The government had given us assurances that satisfied us that we could conduct a free Assembly. The church—in keeping with the courtesy gestures of the nation—had invited the President to attend and to bring a greeting. Had we been scheduled to be hosted by a church in Russia or in China, with promises of freedom for discussion would there have been any theological reason for objecting to a greeting by Prime Minister Kozygin or by President Mao Tse Tung?

Is the church ever justified in withdrawing its witness from an arena of action because the situation is not to its liking? What we are and do and say in a given situation makes the effective witness, but not withdrawal. Governments may censure one another by actions of withdrawal, but is this an arrow in the church's quiver? Certainly we have made no impression on the Brazilian government by our action. We have brought only pain and sorrow to the Brazilian church. In the ecumenical world we have received both censure and commendation. Looking to the future, what is the fine line that determines a decision that will issue in an effective Christian witness? Some of the churches whose delegations would have been decimated had we met in Brazil were represented at the Central Committee meeting of the World Council of Churches in 1967 when it met in Crete. Then, too, there were many protests because of the torture of prisoners by the Greek government, but there were no defections in attendance.

Some who protested our meeting in Brazil stated that they would not attend for fear of bringing reprisals against the Brazilian church. But who other than the Brazilian church should make this decision? President Karl Gottschald of the

21

Brazilian church responded to this point of view with true New Testament conviction. I quote from a letter of his: ". . . we are thankful for your readiness to spare our church unpredictable and evil consequences. But with equal emphasis we must maintain that all of us, members of the Lutheran family and the whole earth, who are to meet for the first time in the Third World and that under the theme of 'Sent into the World', dare not evade confrontation and dialog just to avoid the risks that may have to be taken."

The theme of our Assembly would have confronted us with intensified realism in our discussions had we met in the Brazil of today. In my judgment, the change of location has forfeited a great opportunity. We will now appear to some in the non-believing world as a people who meet only where we can be assured of maximum security and a government to our tastes. But in trust in the Lord of the church, who can make all things work together for good, let us in faith and anticipation address ourselves to the tasks of this Assembly. This afternoon Dr. Appel will present further information about what led up to the decision to meet here in Evian. There will then be opportunity for questions and discussion. But let our discussion be directed toward healing and not to the exacerbation of feelings. Perhaps we can help one another so that in the future in comparable situations we may see more clearly the way we should go.

We thank the Evangelical Churches of France for their willingness on short notice to serve as hosts. And to the staff that has carried out a Herculean logistics task in making it possible for us to meet here in Evian, we owe an incalculable debt of gratitude!

There are 32 youth sitting in this Assembly as voting delegates. No demand came from the youth for this representation. The decision was initiated and voted by the Executive Committee. In the Church of Jesus Christ we are neither male nor female, neither young nor old, but each delegate is responsible under God to the church he represents and to the convictions the Holy Spirit may give him.

A Quick Backward Glance

Many of you are attending an LWF convocation for the first time. If this Assembly is to have some sense of continuity, a brief backward look will be helpful.

There were wounds to be bound up after World War II—colossal tasks of rehabilitation. Through this great need God summoned representatives of Lutheran churches of the world to gather at Lund, Sweden, in July, 1947. There we fashioned the instrument which we call the Lutheran World Federation.

The Assemblies of the past have been deeply concerned with the global needs of each successive era. God has fed this concern through the theology of the church. Who can forget the ringing words of President Anders Nygren at the

Hannover Assembly: "The things which Luther produced by his labors do not lie behind us in the past, but in front of us, very far in front. Luther is not obsolete, but very far ahead of us. In fact, he is so far ahead that we have to expend serious efforts even to locate him and then work vigorously to catch up with him. The Reformation is not an end, but a beginning".[1]

The Minneapolis Assembly of 1957 called for exploratory work looking to dialog with the Roman Catholic Church.

In its theological work this Assembly has been identified as the one where we learned to "think together". Its five chapters of thetical statements on the theme, "Christ Frees and Unites", are probably the strongest pan-Lutheran articulation of what we believe since the time of the Reformation. We who are convened here at Evian would do well in our sectional work not to overlook what we said at the Federation Assembly thirteen years ago.

The Helsinki Assembly of 1963 has been called the "worshiping Assembly". It focused attention on the meaning of justification. A lively discussion followed and time did not permit reconciliation of nuances in interpretation in the plenary sessions. The prepared document, "Justification Today", was referred to the Commission on Theology for editing in light of the group and plenary discussions. This edited document sets forth in a series of twenty-eight paragraphs an explication of justification for modern man in today's world. It should be particularly helpful to Section I of this Assembly.

The Biblical Background for Our Theme

We are assembled under the theme, "Sent Into the World". Much prayer and committee work went into the selection of this theme. The words are a paraphrase of the 18th verse in the 17th chapter of the Gospel according to John. Does this thematic phrase quicken your imagination? Recall the setting. It was Maundy Thursday evening. The New Testament covenant had been invoked by our Lord. In a moving prayer that reviews the meaning of his coming into the world and reaches out to encompass God's purpose for all future generations, he pours out his heart to his heavenly Father. In this 18th verse with which we are concerned, Jesus transfers his own mission to the disciples: "As thou didst send me into the world, so I have sent them into the world" (John 17:18).

It is clear that Jesus' mind was seized with this commissioning of his disciples. And they were not allowed to forget it. The evening of the first Easter Day he reaffirmed what had been said in the prayer on Maundy Thursday evening in the upper room. The disciples were gathered behind locked doors because of fear. With a concern that the disciples be released from fear, Jesus announced, "Peace be with you." Then followed a repetition of the upper room mandate: "As the Father has sent me, even so I send you" (John 20:21).

---

[1] *Proceedings of the Second Assembly of the Lutheran World Federation, Hannover, Germany, 1952*, p. 49.

23

There are two Greek words used in the New Testament for *sent: pempein* and *apostellein. Pempein* emphasizes being sent to accomplish a given task, "the end for which one is sent is indicated"; *apostellein* is the Greek word for "a delegate, a messenger, one sent forth with orders".[2] In both the 17th and 20th chapters of John the word *apostellein* is used. It is clear that Jesus was sending his disciples out under a commissioning, under orders.

It is significant that the tense be noted in Jesus' language. In the 17th chapter he reports the sending as completed: ". . . I have sent them". In the 20th chapter he looks to the future and speaks in the present tense: ". . . I send you". It is obvious that Jesus called his disciples with the intent that they should be commissioned for witnessing and that this was to be a life vocation.

In Jesus' prayer his mind reaches out beyond the small band of disciples: "I do not pray for these only, but also for those who are to believe in me through their word" (John 17:20). Fellow delegates, we are a part of the company who believe in Jesus because of the Word proclaimed by the Twelve and their long succession of witnesses. This truth makes our Assembly theme more than a decorative phrase. It places us under orders of the risen Lord. Indeed, the whole family of God lives constantly under this mandate.

The Content of Our Witness

To be sent presupposes that something is to be transmitted. In the post-resurrection commissioning, Jesus provides instruction as to what is to be transmitted. He declares: "As the Father has sent me, even so I send you". All that Jesus was and said forms the content for everything the church must transmit from generation to generation.

If the content of message is Jesus, we are required to focus our attention on him. The Jesus who was sent by the Father proclaimed forgiveness to the penitent; and by word and deed God's love was boldly expounded. In the story of the Pharisee and the tax-collector, we see a man who could do no better than to blurt out: "God, be merciful to me, a sinner!" (Luke 18:13). But he was pronounced justified. The church is the fellowship of such people.

The forgiven sinner is commissioned to invest his life in good works. In Paul's Epistle to the Ephesians, this is heavily underscored. After a triple emphasis on the truth that we are saved by grace (2:5-9), the apostle declares that we have been saved that we might be free to walk in good works (2:10).

It was this freedom to go "about doing good" (Acts 10:38) that was so fully demonstrated in Jesus' life. No wonder Dietrich Bonhoeffer called Christ a "man existing for others".[3] A friend of mine once asked a Mohammedan scholar to

---

[2] Joseph H. Thayer, *Greek-English Lexicon of the New Testament* (New York: American Book Co), p. 68.

[3] Dietrich Bonhoeffer; *Letters and Papers from Prison* (New York: Macmillan Co), p. 179.

differentiate between the Christian faith and Mohammedanism. His simple reply was: "You have Jesus."

The Christian church is the fellowship of those who have Jesus. Concerning this reality, the Helsinki Assembly's document on justification declared: "The Church is not the fellowship of those who are righteous in themselves and have separated themselves from the world. It is the fellowship of sinners who have received grace. Like its Lord, it lives among sinners, eats and drinks with them and concerns itself with their needs. The members of the Church cannot turn away from the world. They are called in Christian fellowship to sacrifice themselves for the world even if the world is not interested." [4]

He Sends Us Into the World

From the moment the Executive Committee selected the theme for this Assembly, it was unanimous in the conviction that the emphasis was to be placed on the phrase *Into the World*.

Too often the Lutheran Church has been identified with the image of Peter reflected on the Mount of Transfiguration. He wanted to live far from the madding crowd in the company with Jesus, Moses, and Elijah (Matt. 17:4; Mark 9:5; Luke 9:33). This attitude, refusing to be sent, might be religious, but it is a perversion of the gospel.

The New Testament speaks of the *world* frequently. The Greek word *kosmos*, which we translate *world*, in its original meaning from Homer on down, meant "an apt and harmonious arrangement or . . . order".[5] But the New Testament does not use this meaning. After the age of the Ptolmies *kosmos* came to mean "the earth; the inhabitants of the earth, men, the human race; the ungodly multitude; the whole mass of men alienated from God; worldly affairs; the whole circle of earthly goods . . . riches, pleasures which seduce from God and are obstacles to the cause of Christ".[6] It is in one or all of these latter meanings that the New Testament uses the word *world*. In Jesus' prayer the context suggests that the word *world* refers to the inhabitants of the earth, the whole human race.

The World of Today: The Individual

In Bishop Hanns Lilje's keynote address to the Minneapolis Assembly in 1957, he characterized the world of that day as a world of dread *(Angst)* and fear; a world that had witnessed great changes wrought by modern technology; and a world of deep-seated intellectual and spiritual insecurity.[7] Now, thirteen years

---

[4] *Justification Today,* published by the Lutheran World Federation, 1965, p. 7.
[5] Thayer, op.cit., p. 356.
[6] ibid., p. 357.
[7] *Messages of the Third Assembly,* Minneapolis (Minneapolis: Augsburg Publishing House, 1957), pp. 12-13.

later, these descriptive characteristics continue to be valid. In fact, it would not be unfair to say that our awareness of the substance to which they point has been intensified.

Rollo May, one of America's leading psychotherapists, in a current book that some have designated his masterpiece, declares that the problem of people today is "emptiness". It is a time of the "disordered will". Our age is described as a "schizoid world". By the use of this term he means "out of touch; avoiding close relationships; the inability to feel".

Although current permissiveness has thrust upon society extreme freedom in sexual matters, Mr. May finds that "internal anxiety and guilt have increased". He adds: "And in some ways these are more morbid, harder to handle, and impose a heavier burden upon the individual than external anxiety and guilt".[8]

This age, with its overload of problem-beset people, may be God's transmitter of prevenient grace. Mr. May observes: "It is an obvious fact that when an age is torn loose from its moorings and everyone is to some degree thrown on his own, more people can take steps to find and realize themselves".[9]

A man has begun to find himself when he *comes to himself.* It was this Jesus said of the prodigal son. His self-awareness, the recognition of emptiness, provides the sensitivity for alert listening to Jesus' promise: "And this is eternal life, that they know thee the only true God, and Jesus Christ whom thou hast sent." (John 17:3).

How modern man makes the leap of faith, the commitment of trust in Jesus Christ, lies in the mystery of the Holy Spirit's still, small voice. In Bishop Gustaf Aulén's book; *Dag Hammarskjöld's White Book: An Analysis of Markings,* he finds Dag Hammarskjöld's profile of faith in the growing "Yes" in his life. In 1961 Hammarskjöld recorded in *Markings:* "Some moment I did answer *Yes* to Someone or Something—and from that hour I was certain that existence is meaningful and that, therefore, my life, in self-surrender, had a goal." I feel with Bishop Aulén that this *Someone* to whom Hammarskjöld made his commitment was none other than Jesus Christ.

Martin Luther reminds us that as each man must die for himself, so he must believe for himself. Each man's faith, therefore, carries a profile all its own.

The questions related to sharing the good news of the gospel with individuals in today's world will be the concern of those of you who are assigned to work in Section I of this Assembly.

---

[8] Rollo May, *Love and Will* (New York: W. W. Norton & Co., 1967), pp. 28, 16, 41 respectively.
[9] ibid., p. 17.

The World of Today: The Lutheran Church and Ecumenical Commitment

Section II of the Assembly is concerned about ecumenical commitment. The major decisions of Vatican II have been made since the Helsinki Assembly. Dialog between various confessions is going on at international, regional and local levels. Whether it is acknowledged or not, historical walls of separation are beginning to crumble.

Apart from what is happening in today's world, the concern about ecumenical commitment is imposed by the biblical context of our theme. In verse 20 our Lord prays: "I do not pray for these only, but also for those who are to believe in me through their word, that they may all be one; even as thou, Father, art in me, and I in thee, that they also may be in us, so that the world may believe that thou hast sent me."

Lutherans are often nervous in the presence of this prayer. Some of their interpretations have tended to neutralize its meaning by an overemphasis on the spiritual. Other Christians have used John 17:20 as an underpinning for the argument favoring one world-wide church organization. Avoiding either of these polarizations, let us face an obvious fact. Our Lord expected Christian unity to be a means of witness "so that the world may believe that thou hast sent me". This expectation compels one to conclude that the unity our Lord anticipated was to be something the world could recognize.

At the Minneapolis Assembly we spoke with great clarity on the unity of the church in Christ: "Men reconciled to God are one in Jesus Christ. Charged with the ministry and the message of reconciliation, the Church herself is the first fruit of reconciliation: by baptism we are made a people with a life together, a communion, a body, the body of Christ.

Thus her unity is found and founded in Jesus Christ. Neither by ideals nor by enthusiasm, neither by tolerance nor by agreement, are we made one—but by Jesus Christ. In all our attempts to manifest the unity of the Church in visible church fellowship, the dimensions should be neither smaller nor greater than the dimensions Christ has given his Church.

As the communion of reconciliation the Church suffers under her dividedness. We may find some consolation but no excuse in referring to an invisible unity of all true believers. We know that the ministry of reconciliation is jeopardized by the lack of manifested unity.

In this situation the Lutheran Churches are called back to their Confession: "To the true unity of the Church it is enough to agree concerning the doctrine of the Gospel and the administration of the Sacraments; nor is it necessary that human tradition, that is, rites or ceremonies instituted by man, should be everywhere alike." Here the words "it is enough" witness to our freedom: Wherever we hear

27

the gospel preached in its truth and purity and see the Sacraments administered according to the institution of Christ, there we may be assured that the one Church of Christ is present. There nothing separates us from our brethren, and both faith and love constrain us to overcome our dividedness." [10]

At the Third International Ecumenical Seminar at the Lutheran World Federation Ecumenical Center in Strasbourg, France, in August of 1969, the group considering the unity of the church asked itself several questions, one of which was "the form of unity we seek". It was concluded: "The form of unity can be considered only when one has analyzed the church's present situation and has attempted to comprehend the Lord's will concerning unity in this situation. We came to the conclusion that (in view of spiritual life) to an even greater extent we must do those things together which we can do together; and that because of various concepts of the One Truth, we must do those things divided which we cannot yet do together. The unanimity and cooperation in diaconate work must not be dependent on the state of unanimity on the question concerning truth. Diaconate service is thus not to be understood as a means of Christian conversion, but simply as following Jesus." [11]

The World of Today: Responsible Participation in Society

Section III in this Assembly's agenda will give its attention to responsible participation in today's society.

We are sent into this world of our day—in all its moods and needs. Our calling is to serve our neighbor in whatever situation he may find himself. "We are called to translate love and compassion into the structures of justice. In matters of civil liberties and racial integration, of concern for the uprooted and for people in areas of rapid social change, and of care for the mentally and physically disabled, our love fails if it does not materialize in recognition of human rights." [12]

Human rights are continually being violated through white racism. While racism is not a white monopoly, in today's world it asserts itself more generally among white people than among other races. At the Central Committee meeting of the World Council of Churches at Canterbury, England, in August of 1969, considerable attention was given to racism as a world-wide cancerous phenomenon. An Asian theologian of recognized stature told me in vehement language that the acute expression of racism is most prevalent in countries that have had the longest exposure to the Christian gospel. The indictment is true and I shall never forget the depth of feeling with which he made this indictment. Preceding this Assembly our youth participants conducted a conference that gave its attention

---

[10] *Messages of the Third Assembly,* op.cit., pp. 105-106.

[11] Mimeographed report on the Third International Ecumenical Seminar, held at and published by the Ecumenical Research Institute, Strasbourg, France (p. 13).

[12] *Messages of the Third Assembly,* op.cit., pp. 113-114.

to world hunger. There are pockets of poverty in Europe and North America; but in Asia, Africa and Latin America there are huge segments of the population which are undernourished, and in some instances there is chronic starvation. The nations on these continents are eager to use the assistance that industrialization provides; but development capital comes only in trickles. And while they wait for capital, the Western countries use up raw resources. Paul Ehrlich, professor of biology at Stanford University in California, says that "American industrial plans alone envision use of nearly all the noncommunist world's mineral reserves by the year 2000".[13]

One of the phenomenal postwar happenings is the world-wide burgeoning of our cities. And cities are in turn clustering to form megalopoli. Under such congested living, violence and crime thrive; pollution of water and air increases rapidly. Sheer terror is reflected in the prognosis of scientists who give this earth one hundred more years as a habitable place for man.

In this welter of problem issues that have fastened themselves on today's world, how do we go about being "little Christs", sent into the world? Is it not easier for the church to bury its talent? The Minneapolis Assembly did not say *Yes* to temptation. It concluded: "The church is called to enter into the life of each age, to penetrate its thinking, to feel with it in its excitements and torments, and thus to administer God's healing power with precision and compassion. For her obedience to be effective, the church must boldly face the massive revolutionary facts of our time." [14]

The youthful in years will feel a magnetic attraction to this aspect of witness. Some may even regard responsible witness as requiring a turning away from all that is old—yes, to brush it aside. In the presence of such temptation it may not be amiss to recall an observation by Dr. George Forell: "Luther escaped Utopianism because he saw the focus of man's problem in man, not in his environment." [15]

Those of us who are beyond the years of youth find it easy to dismiss social concern with the phrase, "the social gospel". Let us examine this objection in terms of an illustrative area of today's society, namely, national and international relations.

Christians who object to the church's involvement in international affairs usually do so on the basis of Romans 13:1-7. But the context of this section must not be overlooked. Beginning with chapter 12, Paul launches an eloquent appeal for the redeemed person to invest his life in deeds of love. He becomes illustratively specific. In the 13th chapter his specifications point to the Christian's relationship

---

[13] *International Herald Tribune*, December 16, 1969.
[14] *Messages of the Third Assembly*, op.cit., p. 111.
[15] George W. Forell, "Justification and Eschatology in Luther's Thought", a lecture given at a theological conference in Wittenberg, DDR on the occasion of the 450th anniversary of the Reformation.

to the state. The first seven verses make it clear to the Christians in Rome that being a Christian does not exonerate a person from his responsibilities as a citizen of the state. Piety and faith are not an authorization for withdrawal from life.

Indeed, the responsibility of citizenship covers a much larger area today than what was true in Paul's time. Professor Nils Dahl of Yale University has properly observed: "In a situation in which Christians find themselves co-responsible for the order of society, social and political questions . . . take on a significance which they neither had nor could have had in the New Testament period." [16]

The Christian's daily life is lived in the secular kingdom. It is here that he sustains his relationship to other people and to community life. This is the realm in which he must make his ethical decisions, but it is never easy. Evil is an objective reality in the world. It cannot be eradicated, but it must not be suffered supinely, permitting it to have a field day. Lest this happen, it must be fought continually. In doing this the Christian will use the best insights that obedience and reason provide.

In this struggle the Christian will be alert lest he become an idealist unaware of his own finiteness. Man is limited by the place of his calling, the age in which he lives, the particular problems that afflict his generation, his own skills and the capacity of his reason, and the power of evil. The Christian will be optimistic about carrying out God's injunctions to subdue the earth, but he is realistic about accomplishing this task with his own power.

The church is the people of God in the world—a people organized into institutions in society. The people of God live consciously in the world and carry a responsibility to be concerned about justice and the good of all people. Therefore, the church accepts the role of constructive criticism of the state in order that the aims of the state may be furthered. But in doing this, the church never uses the power of the sword and it must always be open to acknowledge its own sin and prejudice. To do this openly before the world is in itself a witness to the truth.

I now return to where we began. The Father sent his Son into the world—this I believe!

The Son sent the disciples into the world. The Son has sent *us* into the world. This I believe! And he who has sent us lives to make intercession for us (Heb. 7:25). In his name the work of this Assembly will be established!

---

[16] Nils A. Dahl, "Is there a New Testament basis for the Doctrine of the Two Kingdoms?", *Lutheran World*, Vol. XII, No. 4, 1965, p. 354.

HEINZ EDUARD TÖDT

Creative Discipleship in the Contemporary World Crisis

I. The history of humanity as theological dimension of the message of justification.

The modern world as it is structured now is basically a world of crises; it does not of itself have any secure, reliable consistency. Its civilization needs careful regulation, planning and development by man. As soon as this does not succeed, as soon as means are misdirected, as soon as war and social injustice disturb and block progress, an awareness of danger arises. That is happening today, as a new wave of crisis-consciousness spreads.

No one who feels the co-responsibility for the future of mankind can extricate himself from this consciousness of crisis. It is not a sign of weakness, but of alertness, that world-wide Christianity is disturbed and asks what it owes to mankind in this situation. In answer to this question different attitudes show themselves. Within Christianity today on all continents, two opposing tendencies are obviously struggling with one another. Sharply polarized, they often reject each other's justification for existence.

One side demands that the Christian churches should undergo a radical conversion to the world and devote all of their resources to actions for change. The premise is that the churches should shift to revolutionary action in order ultimately to be absorbed and lose themselves within their respective societies. Not self-preservation, but only total self-sacrifice would do justice to the church's commission, and make room for the true righteousness of the kingdom of God.

The other side says: Even if the churches as minority groups should actually succeed in humanizing life patterns at the price of sacrificing themselves, they still would not do justice to their commission. For the task which issues from Christ's commission always transcends whatever can be realized by men. The church must therefore, in solidarity with the world, stand critically over against the world—otherwise it inevitably conforms to this world and it cannot be the salt of the earth and mediate the hope which transcends all that has been accomplished in this world. Only by reaching out beyond this world will it be able to keep alive the question concerning the true humaneness of man.

This polarization will, of course, be recognized by most of us as posing false alternatives. Modernity makes progress and change the supreme law. In contrast, tradition seeks to guarantee the particularity, identity and integrity of the churches. If these two are not to end up in false opposition to one another, we must show how a critical and actual appropriation of tradition can yield answers to the questions which the imminent future puts to us.

31

This task already became apparent in 1963 at the last Assembly in Helsinki. The Message of the Assembly declared: [1] The starting point of Luther's Reformation, namely the question, "How can I find a gracious God?" is no longer the question of men today. Man in the modern world questions in a more radical, more elementary way, for his life situation is different. He no longer suffers the burden of his sin, but from the meaningless of existence; therefore, he asks if God has any reality whatsoever. To force man to Luther's starting point would mean to place upon him an alien burden, to place him under a law which will break him. What consequences for the word and action of the Reformation churches have been drawn from this insight?

In 1966 Gerhard Gloege formulated a very decisive thesis.[2] He showed that Luther himself acknowledged that the question, "How can I find a gracious God?" was a distorted, false, abysmal question, because he, the questioner, was negated in his life by the answer he received from God. Only when we orient ourselves to God's question do we begin to think and act theologically. This question is: "How can I get that which I have created back again?" Only this point of view is fundamental: How does God get at his world, his creation, his own? Bonhoeffer expressed it in his letters from prison in this way: [3] How is the world, that has come of age, challenged through Jesus Christ? The lordship of God, the kingdom of God is actualized where the will of God enlists human beings in his service and leads the world beyond that which is inherent in itself.

Theology, therefore, must speak about God's final eschatological will for this world. God's will, however, is discernible only in Jesus and in the powers which have been given to mankind through Jesus for fulfilling this will creatively. Luther's starting point, "How can I find a gracious God?" dare not be used, therefore, as the leading motif either for theology or for preaching. It is far too much the question of an isolated monk, of his deeply anxious conscience, for which nothing matters other than his own eternal salvation. Under the accusation and spiritual anxiety of conscience a person becomes individualized. He is driven into isolation which threatens to cut him off from his fellow men. Even the letter to the Romans, the fundamental source of the Reformation, is not oriented to the spiritual anxiety of the individual. It begins with a great accusation against mankind, which in defiance of the wisdom of God is trapped in self-destructive contradictions and is without excuse. Against this universal background, it indicates that justification, forgiveness, faith and love, is also for us. I agree with Gerhard Gloege: The justification which the gospel speaks takes place as human event, as a cosmological event.

This means that we today can conceive of the meaning of reconciliation, and of our personal reconciliation through Christ only if we proceed from the actual

---

[1] *Proceedings of the Fourth Assembly of the Lutheran World Federation, Helsinki, 1963* (Berlin and Hamburg: Lutherisches Verlaghaus, 1965).
[2] Gerhard Gloege, "Die Grundfrage der Reformation—heute", in *Kerygma und Dogma*, Vol. 12, 1966, pp. 1-13.
[3] Dietrich Bonhoeffer, *Letters and Papers from Prison* (London: SCM Press, 1956).

theological question: How is Christ's claim laid upon this world? This world—that does not mean something abstract, or general, but it means the human process in its current, entirely concrete particularity.

This question is definitely not foreign to modern man, even if the individual question about God has slipped from his view. For modern man knows that he is destined to be the subject of human history. He knows that he bears joint responsibility for the outcome of world history. Even though his thinking may be restricted to this world and his orientation strictly anthropological, and even though the foremost question for him may be, "How can I get along with my own existence and my fellow men?"—he still knows that all of these problems are swept into the process of the world as a whole. Mankind is faced with the question of whether it is still capable of having a future, or whether in fighting itself it will be destroyed by hydrogen bombs, biological weapons and chemical agents. That indeed would be the plunge into meaninglessness, something which modern man apprehends as a threat. We can be certain of one thing: the potential for nihilistic self-destruction is growing, both materially and psychologically. In the midst of such dangers we have to proclaim the gospel, a gospel which ends the power of anxiety in this world and gives confident courage for repentance and new life. Christ's death for mankind clearly indicates that the end of world history by collective suicide can not be the final will of God for his creation. In Christ's act of reconciliation a new freedom, a new hope comes to light.

II. Basic characteristics of the present crisis of humanity

Whoever is inspired by Christ's will for reconciliation, and meets the concrete needs of our time thereby enters into discipleship; he attempts in the present time to imitate Christ's service to the world. Certainly this must be a creative discipleship, for the modern world with its pressures and risks demands new, effective answers. These answers must meet the present-day crisis. Therefore it is necessary to analyze the basic characteristics of this crisis as concretely as possible. We intend to do this by looking at the results of the decade which lies behind us, for this decade began with great hope and ended in widespread disappointment or even despondency.

In 1960 the UNO proclaimed a decade of partnership in world development. It was initially successful. It set in motion a great process of rethinking within world public opinion. The conviction began to spread that development toward a universal world society is not just a desirable goal, but a decisive condition for the survival of mankind. More just political and socio-economic structures would have to be developed within an international system if the pent-up potentials for conflict were not to bring about a chain reaction of catastrophes.

The churches also did much to publicize these ideas. Incorporating within it elements of the Second Vatican Council, the encyclical "Populorum Progressio" declared that development is the new name for peace. It placed under severe judgment the structures and conditions of present systems of world commerce. The World Council of Churches' study conference on "Church and Society" at Geneva in 1966, unlike any previous conference, made Christians in the industrialized nations conscious of the needs and demands of the Third World. This was echoed loudly by the World Council of Churches Assembly at Uppsala in 1968. Moreover, the fact that the World Council of Churches and a commission authorized by the Pope joined for the first time in a long-range common effort for world development, can be regarded as an event of significance for all of church history. The first sentence of the report of the Beirut Conference of 1968 says very programmatically: "The major Christian churches of the world are launching together a program in support of world cooperation for development." [4] This sentence is important for two reasons: first, it formulates the clear, joint intention to foster development; but further, it states that the churches are to be understood as parts of a world wide Christian family, i.e., the universality of the Christian commission is put into action. Since 1968, a number of churches have put into practice the recommendations of Uppsala, and have begun to channel part of their budgets to development aid.

All of this must be evaluated as a new departure filled with promise. But we would be guilty of giving rise to rose colored illusions if we did not also portray the set-backs. The Roman Catholic Church is in a serious crisis, the future outcome of which will decide whether the openness to the world, so magnanimously ventured by Pope John XXIII, will really prevail. In the member churches of the World Council, too, a reversal can be sensed: disappointed by the results of the first decade of development, many church members are withdrawing into local and regional isolation. Frequently there has been no success in making the ecumenical tasks relevant to members of local congregations. After effective information and active congregational participation did not really come about in this decade, many are again turning away practically and theologically from the ecumenical task.

This is all happening in a situation which obviously is highly dangerous. For the fact is that the actual per capita gross national product in the developing nations has not risen at all in the last decade. The will of the broad masses to carve out a share of the benefits of civilization has become stronger, the so-called revolution of expectation has made rapid strides forward, but objective progress has for the most part been absent. By 1968 a debt of 47.5 billion dollars lay heavily upon the developing nations, and repayment of the debt was eating up resources for self-help.

Nevertheless not even the famous Pearson Report of 1969, *Partners in Development*,[5] dared to place drastic demands before the rich industrial nations. It

---

[4] *World Development. The Challenge to the Churches.* The Conference on World Cooperation for Development. Copyright by Exploratory Committee on Society, Development and Peace, WCC, Geneva, 1968.
[5] *Partners in Development. Report of the Commission on International Development.* Chairman: Lester B. Pearson (London: Pall Mall Press, 1969).

recommended an increase in public aid for development by industrial nations to .7% of their gross national product by 1975 or in some instances not even until 1980. Still one must say that the Pearson Report was sober and realistic. In the present circumstances, more than .7% from the industrial nations can not be expected. The Pearson Report unfortunately also avoided any mention of the political difficulties of changing unjust and obstructive social structures both in the developing nations and the industrial nations, even though this is a vital problem. Precisely in its sober realism this excellent report makes evident the objective unreasonableness of the present state of affairs; the want of reason which the conference report from Beirut characterized briefly and to the point, when it said: ". . . all Christians bear heavy responsibility for a world in which it can seem 'normal' to spend $150,000 millions a year on armaments, yet difficult to mobilize more than $10,000 millions for the works of economic and social cooperation".[6]

The balance sheet from the last decade is therefore clear. On one hand, technological reason celebrates a triumphal success: Men have been able to free themselves from the earth's gravity and to take the first laboratories for scientific research to another celestial body. For this act of human expansion hundreds of thousands of human brains and hands were ready to work. Technical fantasy transcended every apparent limit set by nature. For this proud demonstration of human power and national self-affirmation all financial and material means were available, just as they have also been invested under the pressure of anxiety in the gigantic military machines as systems of aggression and deterrence. But sufficient means are always lacking when there is need to make the face of the earth somewhat more human, when slums must be cleaned up, when the undernourished masses demand their share of the food, of modern education and social progress, when institutions and structures should be created which make peace and productive international development possible. In the nations' list of priorities, technological expansion and military security are placed first; way down at the bottom are those concerns which serve to eliminate social injustice, create greater areas of freedom, promote partnership in communication between nations, continents and races and provide a comprehensive and humane education.

It is entirely improbable that this deeply inhuman situation will be tolerated for long; on all continents we sense the gathering of explosive forces which will seek to make an end of this intolerable situation. But how will this happen? Will the potentials which are now aiming at destruction be capable of transforming themselves into powers for rebuilding? Or will those powers grow, which know about the demonic nature of force, and which seek an effective transformation of social and international systems in another way?

The question is directed to us as Christians: Can we merely take for granted the destructive self-contradiction in mankind? Can we be satisfied with the theologi-

---

[6] ibid., p. 9.

cal conclusion that this contradiction is an expression of human sin and therefore assume that its evil consequences cannot be eliminated? Can we approve
our governments and political authorities; can we attribute legitimacy to their
power, when we must see that—in spite of all good intentions—what is obviously
necessary and humane is not being done or cannot be done? Can we accept the
autonomy of a world process which obviously tends toward catastrophic
destruction of life so that it becomes questionable whether human civilization
has a future?

III. Criteria for our orientation

1. *Orientation toward a world-transforming reason*

Christians are a minority of the world's population, but they are strongly
represented in the nations which control the resources of science and technology.
The Christian faith is a minority view in the secularized world, including Europe.
If it is to be publicly effective, it must convince the human mind of its truth.
It owes to the world the critical witness that this rational shaping of our present
world situation has become trapped in the power priorities of this world and is
not guided by love as the highest humane criterion. The entrapment of technological rationality in false priorities has produced the deepest crisis in this
world which has come of age.

Dare we direct our attention primarily and preferentially to reason in the scientific form? For the Christian congregation this form of reason often lies beyond
its field of vision. Here one thinks instead that spontaneous action, pragmatic
reasoning and an open heart for one's fellowmen are important. But this prior
assumption, although no doubt correct, is dangerous at a certain level, because
our everyday life has long been permeated by science and technology. Our feelings, reactions and decision-making often unconsciously follow the lead given
by the mass communications media. We must become aware of the great extent
to which science and technology have become dominant powers in our world
and within ourselves, and we must find a new theological orientation in regard
to them.

That these powers are only at the beginning of their dominance is immediately
evident. During his history of about 40,000 years the so-called homo sapiens
has very laboriously gathered vital knowledge for sustaining life. A single
century, namely, the 19th century, was sufficient for doubling the entire sum of
human knowledge. In the fifty years following that, knowledge again doubled.
At the present time accessible human knowledge is estimated to double every
15 years.[7] Whoever has access to this knowledge, whoever can increase it most
quickly and whoever can decide upon criteria for its application—that individual
group or nation is indeed rich and powerful. Herein lies the critical poverty of

---

[7] Georg Picht, *Mut zur Utopie. Die grossen Zukunftsaufgaben* (Munich: R. Piper & Co. Verlag,
1969), p. 74.

the developing nations, which moreover often lose their intelligentsia through emigration, the brain drain. Today, knowledge is not automatically available to all nations. Here in these monopolies, lies also the basis for the predominance of the super-powers. They control the greatest number of scientists, the most powerful educational institutions, the highest investments in education and science.

It is still thought among scientists that rationality and autonomy are the characteristics of science. These characteristics are indeed for the most part appropriate for details in scientific work today: for experimentation and evolvement of theories, for scientific discussion and verification. But the sciences cannot control the application and consequences of their conclusions; the choice of research projects depends upon financial backing, and this is dictated more and more by non-scientific criteria. Space exploration and armaments, economic rivalry and the self-protection of society dictate the priorities according to which science and technology wield their power. Our entire life is infiltrated by the direct and indirect consequences of such claims of priority.

Since Christianity is strongly represented in those nations which have technology and science at their command, it ought to be clear about its own co-responsibility for their consequences. We have to deal with the problem of the priorities according to which science and technology are oriented. For example, whether they serve only the escalation of national power or whether they in fact acknowledge an obligation to strive for development and peace for all mankind. Establishing such priorities can be influenced in many ways: in extended public discussion, by the opinion moulding process among scientists, and above all through the kind of spirit which permeates the educational system. Here will be decided whether the realm of freedom and spontaneity in the future will become smaller, whether men will be dominated by technocratic competition, or whether humane points of view can be made to prevail.

This now is my thesis, which I would strongly underline: today the Christian church has a pivotal co-responsibility to help orientate science toward freedom and humanity. Up to this time, however, it has hardly developed any organs and institutions by means of which it could realize this responsibility, since the churches actually live with a very limited understanding of the implications of science. Theology has for the most part lost its contact with the world-transforming sciences. That is historically an unfortunate development, which today is difficult to correct, because science and technology are advancing at such a terrific rate.

Despite this there are important points at which a realization of this responsibility can begin. This does not mean merely the increase of scientific findings, they are increasing anyhow, but rather it means interpreting them critically and humanely with regard to their significance, their implications and their consequences for society. This must presently be done in three areas: First, by the churches' contribution to world development; secondly, their involvement in peace research; and thirdly, by investigation of social change, which has drawn into its wake both the rural and urban population on all continents, and radically calls into question the previous functions of Christian congregations.

In all of these areas one of the central tasks of critical study is to investigate how vital communication contacts can be established between the base, namely the members and active groups of the congregations, and the totality of ecclesiastical and ecumenical institutions and their tasks. A second central responsibility in all of these areas is to restore theologically the coherence between scientific knowledge and the articulation of faith. Today, theology can become the point of crystallization for many sciences and scientists, if it concretely poses the question concerning human responsibility, if it examines it more intensively than is being done by the positivistic scientific and academic apparatus, and pursues this in carefully conceived scientific projects.

When I think of these tasks, I cannot urge that the church and theology should be absorbed by the world. On the contrary, only a critical distinction from the world, to which Christians are called by the message of the gospel, can enable them to oppose the dominant tendencies of the time and to sensitize the conscience of man concerning the question of true humanity and the future of man. Theology calls reason back to its own particular vocation, when it understands how to give new validity to reason's highest criterion—love for God's creation.

My question about the future orientation of the Lutheran World Federation is this: Will we be in a position to find concrete ways of realizing this co-responsibility for the freedom of science and the criteria of its orientation?

2. The productive significance of the doctrine of the Two Kingdoms

The co-responsibility of Christians in today's concrete crisis is something which I do not derive simply from the current mentality. Instead my thesis is: By creating freedom and love, the gospel affords us criteria with which reason can find its orientation and free itself from false priorities. The reason of which we speak is not reason in the abstract, but in that form which it has assumed through its incarnation in our present, scientific-technological world.

How is that related to the doctrine of the Two Kingdoms, such as is operative in Lutheranism? Does not this doctrine tend to partition off the gospel, the spiritual realm, precisely from all things earthly, and thus relinquish the world to its own self-interests? Does not this doctrine separate the message of love from the necessary ordering of this world and the secular reason which corresponds to it? This kind of static-dualistic use of the doctrine of the Two Kingdoms is unfortunately widespread. Such use is made of it when one advocates conservative quietism in public matters and emphasizes individual salvation in the private realm. But, I am afraid, in doing this one misses completely the truth and sense of the doctrine of the Two Kingdoms and appeals wrongly to Luther. One can conclude this from Luther's own attitude even without complicated theological investigation. Luther certainly opposed mixing together the spiritual and secular realms. He fought clericalism as strongly as he fought religious authorization of secular-political offices or of political action. For example, he felt that he could not tolerate for this reason the peasants who proclaimed their revolt in Christian terms as a concern of the gospel.

Luther felt obligated as a doctor of theology to enter into the secular events of his time with demands, recommendations and advice and to remind Christians of their specific responsibility. From them, this must be strongly underlined today, he expected non-violence and the waiving of rights in personal matters, strictly corresponding to the requirements of discipleship in the Sermon on the Mount. His theology enabled him to demand publicly a new law of peace as a replacement for the medieval laws governing feuds and the protection of one's own interests. In his exposition of the Magnificat, in 1520-21, he virtually taught the people a lesson in law. He repeatedly demanded the establishment of schools and development of an educational system and interpreted these things to be the proper consequences of evangelical preaching. In the famous "Sermon on Keeping Children in School", from 1530, there is the sentence: "Therefore, to tell the truth, peace, which is the greatest of earthly goods, and in which all other temporal goods are comprised, is really a fruit of true preaching." [8]

If temporal peace is a proper fruit of preaching, there is tied to this ministry of preaching an eminently critical task. It is almost inconceivable to me how it was possible that Luther's sharp, public accusations against the rulers of his time, against "tyranny and suppression" of the poor have been forgotten, and how views in favor of a general and uncritical legitimization of those in power have been derived from Luther's doctrine of the Two Kingdoms.[9] That it has been the subject of so much attention is really only understandable in the light of the tragic event of the Peasant War.

Luther very strictly measured the practical action of rulers over against the gracious will of God and the concrete needs of man according to which both reason and love should function. Politics, law, economics and science—regardless of all distinctions of competence—do not exist for him self-sufficiently in an isolated realm, but need critical instruction. Doing this is the obligation of those who on the basis of renewed thought inquire about what is now the good and perfect will of God (Rom. 12:2). If, therefore, we now orient ourselves according to Luther's own behavior as a competent interpretation of the doctrine of the Two Kingdoms, we will then recognize our obligation toward analogous responsibilities in our own time.

---

[8] Luther's *Works*, Philadelphia edition, Vol. IV, p. 149; *Weimare Ausgabe*, WA 30, 2 538.

[9] Cf., for example, Luther's criticism of princes and lords in his "Admonition to Peace", *Works*, Philadelphia edition, Vol. IV, pp. 219-244; *Weimare Ausgabe*, WA 18, 333.

3. Criteria for true humanity in Jesus' commission

Nothing appears more difficult for present-day theology than a concrete formulation of critieria, based on the gospel, for responsibility toward the world. Reasons for this are inherent in the experience of modern man, of the modern Christian. God's will for us has become deeply hidden from our view. Earlier generations believed that they could derive God's will from the existing orders of creation and the laws of nature. Because of this they spoke freely of the divine governance of the world. That is no longer possible for us. We know that today man is largely in a position to develop the structures of life in this world and to put entirely new processes into operation. We know that we have to direct all life toward the future and that we ourselves must find its criteria. That is the "coming of age" about which Dietrich Bonhoeffer spoke so impressively.

If previously man's sin consisted of deviation from the existing orders, today we must primarily measure sin according to his failure over against the future. Today sin becomes most clearly evident where man falls short in his task and destiny. Concretely that means: man fails wherever he as the administrator of this earth makes the structures and relationships of this world contradict human dignity and thus permits men to become enemies of one another. If one measures the failure of man according to the task with which he is challenged, theology appears to become radically anthropological, since everything man does has reference to the future of man in his world and seemingly must be accounted for by man. But it is now evident that the God-question has gained a new dimension. Man, who knows his responsibility for the world, and its future, becomes burdened by the anxiety as to whether he will succeed in doing justice to this responsibility. He sees the destructive contradictions which threaten the fulfillment of his task and he senses that there is need for a new spirit, even a new man, if there is to be a decent future for mankind. Only by means of a world filled with justice, love and humanity is there a positive answer to our initial theological question, "how can God recover his creation, his world?" But only by the renewal of man can the world become new. From what source can we derive hope for such renewal? All experience simply indicates that time and again the world corrupts man and man in turn corrupts the world—a vicious circle in which one evil is the source of the other. Therefore, despair is one's closest companion in soberly viewing the world and meaninglessness is the most likely perspective.

This is the situation to which the gospel speaks. Its first and fundamental statement is not the crushing demand to create a world with better justice. Its first statement is encouragement: God has made a new beginning in Christ. From this beginning arises new life and freedom. Whoever, regardless of appearances, regardless of all he experiences, believes this promise receives new confidence, new hope and can escape from the negative suggestion into which he is lured by the vicious circle of corruption.

Certainly, particularly at this juncture, we cannot and do not want to raise the urgent questions about the success or perversion of man's future less pointedly. We definitely must ask about how those future creatures will look which man will create when his ability to manipulate the genetic code has been further developed. What soul will live in the creatures who will be less and less able to escape from being conditioned by the organization of the social milieu and who at the same time must bear and reflect the destructive contradictions and antagonism of this organization.

But we Christians do not question aimlessly, as though groping in the dark for the future image of man. We know about criteria which are indispensable if the image of man is to remain that of a true human being. Our quest for the future man orients itself to him whom the gospel calls the final, the eschatological man, the first born among the sons of God. In Jesus and his destiny the image of true, perfect man stands before us; from him criteria shine forth which should direct our search for the image of the future man for whom we are responsible.

In the story of the temptation in Matthew the great temptations of mankind appear as prophetically anticipated. After forty days and nights of fasting and hunger, Jesus is approached by the tempter. He suggests to him that he help himself by turning stones into bread. He offers him the power and glory of all kingdoms in this world in order to divert him from the way that lies before him, namely, the way of suffering. Jesus rejects this. All of the self-help, power and glory of man will only bring forth a satanic world, if in its midst this one thing does not remain: the life of sacrifice for others, of suffering with one's neighbor which brings us closer to him, even closer than any common action. In going to the cross, Jesus accepted God's will, because productivity, self-realization, joy are all in vain, if at the center of the world there would not be the vicarious suffering which frees man from the bonds with which he is tied to himself and also from the coercion of activity. Here the truth emerges toward which all other criteria of man's humanity must be oriented if there is to be new hope for the future of the human race. Responsibility for the world, which arises from faith, will be guided by true compassion. It will struggle toward the end that suffering in this world be lessened by every means at the disposal of modern man, and that the willingness to serve as Jesus' disciples be extended throughout the world. It seems to me that, in the final analysis, here is the salt without which everything else will quickly spoil.

IV. A concluding comment

A number of practical consequences can be drawn from my lecture. I have already spoken about the new responsibility for the sciences, for their independence and for bringing them into line with humane objectives. Allow me only to express at this time a thought which has often received too little attention in the Lutheranism of the twentieth century. It concerns the dignity of man. Today more than ever before this theme has come into question as a result of racial discrimination, suppression, terror and torture on all continents. Considered from a theological perspective, the dignity of men has been irrevocably established in that Christ has accepted all men as his brothers and has given his life for them. No one stands in greater solidarity with Christ than the man who suffers. We have to examine ourselves, however, as to the weight which the present injuries to the dignity and the rights of our fellowmen (including the ones we ourselves inflict) have for our faith and our conscience. Theologically, these actions must be understood as a desecration of man as the image of God. What is needed is a new sensitivity to that which we as Christians owe to those who suffer from discrimination. We know that the bread necessary for the overcoming of hunger must be provided. But do we know with the same urgency and concreteness that some members of the family of man hunger for something other than bread and nourishment, for actual equality, for actual participation in the basic decisions concerning life and humanity, for respect which protects them from being ruled over and controlled by others, ourselves included? They hunger simply for a real recognition of their human dignity. Only where this hunger is satisfied does the brotherhood before God, to which we have all been called, truly begin.

Translated from the German by Professor Eugene Skibbe, Minneapolis, Minnesota, USA.

KENT S. KNUTSON

The Response of the Lutheran Churches to the Roman Catholic Church and Theology Today

Lutherans and Roman Catholics confront one another today in ways without parallel in our controversial history. The change can be traced to October 1962, the opening of the Second Vatican Council.

Lutherans and Roman Catholics confront one another today in a world dramatically different from that of even a generation ago. The question that faces us now is not only how we should capitalize on the new possibilities for relationships with one another but how we can survive as the church of Jesus Christ in the western world.

The fourth Assembly of the Lutheran World Federation met in Helsinki, Finland, in 1963 before the issuance of the first Vatican II document. This is our first opportunity as a world assembly to speak to Lutheran people and Catholic people concerning the significant events of these intervening years and to assess their effect on our mission to the world.

The present situation harbors both an unhappy fact and a lively hope.

We are separated from one another.

We confess the same Lord, we believe in the same catholic creeds, we recognize and receive baptism as God's holy sacrament, we celebrate the Holy Communion in the faith that we eat and drink Christ's body and blood, we teach and discipline a necessary ministry, we rejoice that we are in the body of Christ in the church, we receive the same forgiveness of sin, we accept the authority of the same Scripture, we pray for the guidance of the same Holy Spirit and we look for God's consummation. Despite all this, we are separated one from the other. Sometimes caused by misunderstanding and accompanied at times by hostility, the gulf of separation yawns deep and wide.

Yet we are hopeful that this separation can be overcome.

A long history combined with the stresses of a critical age weigh us down. Despite this, our conviction is that an age of new understanding has dawned which promises opportunities for new relationships between us.

The story of our separation begins nearly half a millennium ago. A young university student is caught in a thunderstorm. Lightning strikes and he cries in terror, "St. Anne, help me! I will become a monk!" Thus begins for Martin

43

Luther a career which shakes the church and creates forces which have haunted us with both joy and sorrow until this very day. His search for and discovery of clarity in the gospel, his attempts to bring about reform in the church, his own ex-communication from his church, the writing of new confessions claiming truth and catholicity for the Christian communities in his land culminate in the creation of a separate church called, unfortunately, the Lutheran Church.

Inexorably history marched on—the council of Trent in which the differences were solidified, the onset of the Counter-Reformation, the definition and refinement of theological differences and customs and procedures and even the shedding of blood.

Thereafter the Lutheran and Catholic churches lived through the common history of the western world—the rise of modern science, the development of the new world, a great missionary movement, the industrialization of our nations and wars—many wars of enslavement and liberation. But each went its own separate way. Each experienced dry periods and exalted periods, growth, recession, renewal in the ensuing centuries but no bridging of the separation.

Signs of hope arose as the two churches entered the twentieth century. Those churches spawned by the sixteenth century reformation struggled for new relationships with one another and brought into being an ecumenical movement which included the great church of the east. But the Roman Catholic Church stood aloof.

The second chapter of the story begins when the fathers of the Roman Catholic Church gathered in St. Peter's in Rome for the Second Vatican Council.

It is a long time from 1520 to 1962.

God will not give us as much time to conclude this second chapter.

"In this assembly", the Council said, "under the guidance of the Holy Spirit, we wish to inquire how we ought to renew ourselves, so that we may be found increasingly faithful to the gospel of Christ. We shall take pains so to present to the men of this age God's truth in its integrity and purity so that they may understand it and gladly assent to it." [1] Impelled by the love of Christ, they kept before them "those who still lacked the opportune help to achieve a way of life worthy of human beings." [2]

The assembly in St. Peter's achieved more in the next four years than had been planned or perhaps even dreamed. Responding to the call of Pope John XXIII to

---

[1] *The Documents of Vatican II*, Walter M. Abbott, S.J. General Editor (New York; Guild Press, 1966); "Message to Humanity", pp. 3-4.

[2] ibid., p. 5.

open the windows of the church, the Council explored many areas of faith and life. Through intense and open debate they forged a new direction for their church and for the whole people of God.

This Council constitutes a challenge to the Lutheran Church unprecedented in our history and equalled in importance only by the challenge of a hostile world.

I. The Second Vatican Council

Our reaction to this Council is different than to the two intervening Councils since the Reformation. We rejoice in this Council and thank God for it.

We interpret this Council to be the end of the Counter-Reformation. Instead of our two churches pitted against each other, there now exist mutual efforts to strengthen one another and to discover ways of recognizing and relating to one another.

We interpret this Council to be not only the end of one age but the beginning of a new age—a new participation by the Roman Catholic Church in the search for reconciliation of all Christians.

We interpret this Council to be the dynamic which institutes renewal in the church, in faith, in worship, in clarity in doctrine, in church government, in life in the world and in mission to the world.

We interpret this Council to be a new definition of the role of the church in the modern world, identifying with the needs of all mankind and accepting the fact of change and its influence on the life and thought of the church.

The Council produced sixteen documents which are a fertile field for research for years. We cannot comment on all of them. Many bridges across the chasm of separation were built. Five of them are of special interest.

1. *The Concept of the Church*

The expansive exposition on the doctrine of the church is the most significant achievement of the Council. The description of the church in the biblical language of people of God speaks to us clearly and we hear the theme of self-correction and self-criticism which marks a pilgrim church. The dynamic of the church does not lie in its structure or management but beyond human merit in God himself. The emphasis on the collegial character of the church, reminiscent of both patristic and reformation thought, is a welcome one to us. The use of the biblical theme of the general priesthood of all believers is as though we were speaking ourselves. The universal call to holiness and the attention paid to the relation between the church militant and the church triumphant inspires us also to examine ourselves.

2. Scripture and Tradition

The treatment of the relation between Scripture and tradition is of special interest to us. It is no secret that we were troubled by the language which stated that there were two sources of revelation which seemed to lie side by side. The clarity with which the Council speaks of Christ the Word, the history of Israel, the obedience of faith by which man entrusts his whole self freely to God, the transmission of this Word in the written Word inspired by the Spirit, and the preaching of the Word in its purity, inspired by the same Spirit assists us greatly in understanding present Roman Catholic teaching. The injunction to read the Scripture directed to all the faithful and especially to those who preach is like hearing our own Reformation come to life.

The meaning of tradition for the Catholic is not as clear to us. We know that we ourselves have not always recognized the complex relation between tradition and Scripture and we have learned, with other Christian brethren in the assemblies of Faith and Order, to examine this in greater depth.

3. Worship

The renewal of worship and its forms has not been confined to the Roman Catholic Church nor the Vatican Council. We rejoice that worship received so much attention from the Council. A striking feature is the emphasis that Scripture has paramount importance in the liturgy. The restoration of preaching in the service on the theological basis that Christ is present not only in the sacraments but also "in His word, since it is He Himself who speaks when the holy Scriptures are read in the church",[3] reminds us of our language of "means of grace" and provides a new dimension to our understanding of Catholic teaching. The priesthood of believers is again emphasized with the requirement that the faithful take part knowingly, actively and fruitfully in worship. The use of the vernacular, the growth of hymn singing, as well as the commending of private devotions bring our people together as never before. It is disappointing to us that the question of individual masses is not dealt with more clearly and that the chalice is still not permitted to the laity except in special instances.

4. Relations with Other Churches

The stride forward by the Council in recognizing "ecclesial communities" outside of the Catholic Church is of enormous importance. We hope that this prepares the way for the next step—full recognition that we are a true church. The Council also confirms a fundamental principle of both the Reformation and the twentieth century ecumenical movement that renewal and reform are essential to the recovery of the visible unity of the church. The indication that "both sides were to blame"[4] demonstrates the new atmosphere in which we move in our relationships.

---

[3] ibid., p. 141: Paragraph 7 in "Constitution on the Sacred Liturgy".
[4] ibid., p. 345: Paragraph 7 in "Decree on Ecumenism".

We are sorry that the Catholic Church still finds it necessary to say "it is through Christ's Catholic Church alone, which is the all-embracing means of salvation, that the fullness of the means of salvation can be obtained".[5]

5. *The Role of the Church in the World*

The designation by the Council of the servant role of the church is of great consequence. We who are gathered here in Evian to discuss the theme, "Sent Into the World", can learn much from this. The "Declaration of Religious Freedom" is singularly and dramatically significant to Protestants. It clarifies questions and concerns which we have carried for centuries. The positive attitude toward the world is a good antidote to the negativism which we ourselves sometimes display. The social character of man's life which the Council emphasizes is a corrective for the extreme individualism sometimes fostered among Lutherans.

Many questions remain, but the solid base of common understanding on these items is clearly communicated by Vatican II.

II. The Post-Council Theology and Church

Not yet five years have passed since Vatican II. This is insufficient time to come to any clear conclusion concerning the full effect of the conciliar decisions. However, it is not too early to claim that the influence on the life and thought of the Catholic Church has already been far-reaching. The renewal in the worship life has been the most prominent and universal. The vitality of lay movements, steps toward democratization in church government, shifts in methods and emphases in education, changes in many religious orders, and increased contacts with other Christians and with the secular world have contributed to the creation of a dynamic image of the Catholic Church.

Two counter-movements to orderly renewal also are evident. Great impatience is shown by some with vivid challenges to church authority and the formation of the so-called "underground church". Resistance to renewal is still strong in many parts of the world. The decline in the candidates for the priesthood and the religious orders, restlessness among some priests, the defection of many youth and the wide-spread open criticism of the church are evidence of the differing reactions to the rate of change within the Roman Catholic Church.

1. *Developments in Biblical Interpretation*

The return to the use of biblical language in the deliberations of Vatican II is a significant step forward in clarifying communication between Catholics and other Christians. The interest in biblical research in the Catholic Church has continued and grown. The employment of historical tools in biblical research,

---

[5] ibid., p. 346: Paragraph 3 in "Decree on Ecumenism".

the consideration of several theories concerning the origin of the biblical books and the analysis of the inner development of biblical thought has made possible a greater degree of understanding between Lutherans and Catholics. Biblical scholars have found their efforts to be mutually helpful and have come, more and more often, to common results. It is a striking feature of these post-Council years that Lutheran and Catholic scholars through independent work come to the same conclusion in the interpretation of biblical texts. Although there is still controversy in some areas in biblical studies, the spectrum of discussion is as wide in the Catholic as in the Lutheran Church.

One of the most important contributions is the discovery of the significance of diversity of thought within the Bible. The biblical writers chose to proclaim the one gospel through a variety of languages, emphases and perspectives. This raises the distinct possibility that there can be a variety of authentic expressions of the faith which faithfully represent particular biblical witnesses to the one truth concerning Jesus Christ. If this is so, the recognition that other Christian traditions have valid and even profound insights into revelation is not only permitted but a direct requirement of fidelity to the authority of Scripture. Lutherans have often been associated with Pauline thought and emphases. Lutherans need to accept Christian communities with Johannine or Matthean or Petrine theologies as being as truly biblical as Paul.

2. *Developments in Theology*

There have always been schools of theology in every church. The field of theological study has thus always been wider than the official teachings of the church. Past Catholic systematic theology, however, had been characterized by adherence to absolutist scholastic categories closely allied to medieval thought. Lutheran theology has often tended to a scholasticism as well but of the post-Reformation period. Communication between the two communities of scholars was difficult and sometimes impossible. Today the situation is quite different. There is a qualitative difference to the work of the present-day theologians. Philosophical bases tended to be firm in the past and the language used clear and definable. Today language is so fluid and the pluralism in philosophy so rampant, the choices therefore so many, that theological thought has burst out of its customary moulds and emerged into new styles of discourse. This at once makes communication more difficult but at the same time puts all theological work on the same plane with increasing recognition of common problems. A new dialogical relationship among theologians has thus arisen to the benefit of all.

It is common place in the theological seminaries in the Lutheran Church for the student to read the books of Roman Catholic theologians as well as those of his own tradition. The names of such prominent Catholic theologians as Karl Rahner and Hans Kung of the German-speaking world, E. Schillebeeckx of Holland, Yves Congar of France, George Tavard of the United States and many others have become very well known among Lutherans.

48

Catholic scholars have been willing to express their faith in language which is not only acceptable but appealing to Lutherans. Catholic thinkers have also been willing to engage in speculative theology as far ranging as the most radical of Protestant theologians. Recent reflections concerning the concept of God, the meaning of universal salvation, the relation of Christian and non-Christian thought, the analysis of and dialog with atheism have been in common in both Lutheran and Catholic circles.

Of special interest to Lutherans has been the publication and wide circulation of *A New Catechism* produced by the Catholic Church in Holland. There can be little doubt that theological thought in the Catholic Church has progressed beyond the Council in such areas as the sacraments, the church, authority in the church, the relation of Scripture and tradition and the role and function of ministry. These developments show Lutheran and Catholic thought to be on a convergent course, bringing us closer together than our definitive theological positions indicate.

Of some concern to us has been the theological direction of Papal Encyclicals. "The Mystery of Faith", published in 1965, restricts the discussion of the mystery of the real presence in the Lord's Supper to the language of transubstantiation as defined by the Council of Trent. This seems to us to be contrary to much opinion in the Catholic Church and proves a hindrance to the achievement of clarity regarding the theology of the Eucharist. The encyclical on "The Transmission of Life" issued in 1968 bases its views on marriage and the control of births, on natural law which it claims the teaching authority of the church is competent to interpret. It further suggests that faithful observance to the interpretation is necessary for man's eternal salvation. This, too, seems quite out of step with a great deal of current Catholic theological thought.

The recent encyclical on "Mixed Marriages" teaches a view of the validity of marriage and the obligation of the Catholic partner to educate the children in the Catholic faith which is not only offensive to us but different than the teaching of many Catholic theologians.

3. Direct Dialogs

Of very great importance has been the mushrooming contacts between Catholic and Lutheran theologians on official and unofficial levels. Even before Vatican II, the Lutheran World Federation at Minneapolis in 1957 established an Institute for Ecumenical Research later situated in Strasbourg, France. Since that time, this Institute has concentrated on research in Catholic theology and dialog with Catholic theologians. Pope Paul VI has sponsored an Ecumenical Institute outside Jerusalem which will bring theologians of many traditions together for dialog. Many other types of institutes and research centers have sprung up all over the world.

Catholic and Lutherans have as well been engaged in an official international dialog. The results of this have not yet become available. One example of a very fruitful work is the official dialog in the United States. Lutheran and Catholic theologians have been working on a series of problems for five years. They have issued the results of their discussion on the Nicene Creed, Baptism, and Eucharist as Sacrifice. These are striking examples of the progress that can be made in our time. The Sacrifice of the Mass has been a critical problem in the relationship between our two churches since the beginning. This dialog shows that it is possible for Lutherans to accept the Catholic view of the Mass when it is communicated in contemporary language and some misinterpretations cleared away. Catholics too can accept the Lutheran understanding of the real presence.

The group in the United States will soon publish the results of their work on the ministry, long considered to be an insoluble problem. This will show that it is possible for a Catholic to accept the Lutheran ministry as a valid ministry as presently constituted. The implications of this are very great. If Catholics can accept the sacraments and the ministry of the Lutheran Church, it follows that they can also accept the Lutheran Church as a true and full church.

4. Lay Involvement

These years have been filled with many contacts between the people of our two churches. Through group meetings in homes, in retreats and in study conferences of many kinds, laymen have confronted one another in such ways as to achieve lasting friendships. Common Bible study, discussion of the Christian life and the sharing of problems of life in the modern world have brought many Lutherans and Catholics to complete acceptance of each other.

College students have not only listened to teachers of the other tradition but have studied the faith together in conferences and small groups leading to the conclusion that they see no reason why they should continue in separate communities of faith. In Dubuque, Iowa, in the United States, my own seminary, Wartburg Theological Seminary; Aquinas Institute, a Dominican Seminary; and Dubuque Seminary, a Presbyterian school of theology, have formed an association of schools which freely interchanges teachers and students. Next year Lutheran and Catholic students will study the introduction to the Bible in a common course of study.

Cooperation among the laity, as well as the clergy, on special projects provides additional avenues for growth in understanding. The involvement in 1967 of the Roman Catholic Church in the United States in the 450th anniversary of the Reformation is a startling example of the new willingness to reexamine those matters which have caused hurt in the past. The common cause which has been made to alleviate social injustice, solving problems in public and private education, helping one another where persecution threatens and many more instances has eradicated old prejudices and created a new trust. Marching in a demonstration to protest racial prejudice has become a new ecumenical method!

The actual life and theology of the two churches has gone beyond anything the official position of the Lutheran Church or even the Vatican Council had envisioned.

III. The Future

The future holds much promise and much work for Catholics and Lutherans. I believe that we are on a convergent course. If history will permit the time, we shall move more closely together. Our goal can be nothing less than reunion. How many generations must pass before we have surmounted the remaining obstacles is known only to God. Surely much will be determined by the faithfulness and the energy with which we handle our responsibilities in this generation. The work which we have begun in these short years must be continued and expanded. Both Catholics and Lutherans will need to change while maintaining faithfulness to the gospel and continuity.

The Lutherans must pick up the challenge issued to them by the events engendered by Vatican II. I have not seen the dynamic renewal among us that we are witnessing among Catholics. I have not been sure that we have committed ourselves to the goal of reunion. We have been active in the ecumenical movement and contributed much to it. This we must also continue and expand to include the so-called Third Force (the Pentecostal churches) with whom we have had little or no contact.

The theological agenda is long and cannot be reviewed here. Surely it calls for deep immersion into the comprehensiveness of the Catholic tradition, for much more sensitivity and understanding of Catholic piety and greater appreciation of the use of symbol in Catholic thought. Even such difficult problems as the Papacy are considerably softened by the realization of their symbolic value. Lutherans are often too literal in their approach to both doctrine and life.

But an even more fundamental question remains. Will history give us enough time? All that we have outlined here assumes that the basic problem lies in the past and that we must somehow "re-do" our past in order to live together in the present. We have assumed that history moves prophetically, that is, one age follows another with clear continuity and that each stage of history grows clearly out of the preceding one. The profound question to ponder is whether we are not living in an apocalyptic age in which God is thrusting us forward by leaps and bounds and calling us to break with our past at numerous points. Renewal may not be reform of that which is but rather radical disjunction of the present so that new types of Christian life emerge which have no parallels in immediate past history. We cannot assume any longer that the predominant expression of the Christian faith will be in the western world. God may be moving his candlestick to other places with dramatically different cultural orientations. If we rely wholly on past history, history may pass us by.

There is little doubt that we face problems in our world which dwarf the luxuries of subtle theological distinctions. If we are serious about being "Sent Into the World" we shall have to look beyond our wealth, our unnecessary traditions, and our culture to the real world in which God asks us now to act.

Our basic problem is not our past but our mission to the present world. We have time to suggest only three critical areas of concern.

1. The Population of the World

It seems clear that unless there is some radical readjustment in history which we cannot foresee, the world's population will double again in the next 35 years. Experts tell us that the energy base on our planet is insufficient to feed, clothe and house this population. Massive starvation will start in 1975, they say, with accompanying social disorder, plunging standards of living and disillusionment beyond anything experienced in the modern age even in times of war. Can the church survive through such a generation? What kinds of shifts in moral values are necessary to cope with a disintegrating world. Surely, this is a problem of such dimension that we can do nothing less than minister to such a world to-gether.

2. Youth Culture

It is also clear that the youth of the world is creating a value system which represents a substantial shift from that which presently predominates in the Christian church. The Age of Aquarius is coming. Recently within the Vatican walls, I was treated to a fascinating conversation concerning the Broadway musical "Hair", which has captivated the younger generation and demonstrates a sense of freedom and a view of man which, if it predominates, will surely usher in a very different kind of Christian community in the next two genera-tions. Youth culture knows of no denominational barriers. It cannot identify with the problems of the past with which we are so captivated in the church today. There are fewer and fewer "Catholic" and "Lutheran" youth. There is rather a vital articulate and sometimes confused youth which is demanding a radical obedience in the Christian life which challenges the comfort of the established churches. Can we prepare the way for our own children to keep the faith within the church?

3. International Disorder

It also seems clear that we cannot assume that the present balance of power will remain in the world. The division between east and west which has domi-nated our lifetime, and the emergence of the ecumenical movement, is no longer the basic political arena in which we conduct our mission. The future most likely does not belong to the white man or to the industrial nations. The culture of other races may well predominate and the basic political problem will become that of the gulf between the have and the have-not nations. The Christian church is identified with the west and with the white man. The change in the international scene will so substantially affect the character of mission that we can do nothing less than face it together.

Grave international disorder with an increase in the number of wars may result from the working out of the new balances of power. The long identification by the church with defense of the present order, even to the point of furnishing the manpower to fight wars with other nations whose churches also furnished manpower, is a problem of such dimensions that the churches must face it with one voice if it is to be surmounted. Can we?

It is to these kinds of questions that we must direct our attention as well as to the agenda we already have before us. We cannot wait long.

The next great Council cannot be "Catholic" or "Lutheran". If world assemblies are possible at all any longer in our kind of world, they will need to include the great Roman Catholic Church whose awakening to renewal and mission challenges us all with its breadth and intensity. Can we hope for a real Ecumenical Council of the kind which Luther demanded?

We are still separated while we live in the faith that we are in the body of Christ. Yet our hope is lively that our separation can be overcome. Perhaps another young university student will show us the way.

JAN WILLEBRANDS

Sent Into the World

It is a great honor and at the same time a great pleasure for me to participate in this most important Assembly of the Lutheran World Federation and to be allowed to make a contribution to its labors. My pleasure is all the greater because I had the good fortune to be present at the contacts between the Roman Catholic Church and the Lutheran World Federation from the very beginning, and the Lutheran-Catholic dialog has thus come to be very close to my heart.

But my pleasure is not merely and indeed not even principally based on personal reasons. Today it has become a matter of course that no church can be indifferent to what happens in another church. The presence of each other's observers at our respective assemblies has thus become a matter of course. But this was not enough for the leadership of your Federation. It has given an even more significant sign of its ecumenical spirit by inviting the President of the Secretariat for Promoting Christian Unity, as the representative of the ecumenical endeavors of the Roman Catholic Church, to address your Assembly. This invitation shows how far our dialog has progressed in the few years that have passed since the Second Vatican Council. In my own name, and also in that of the Holy Father, I therefore want to thank you wholeheartedly for this ecumenical gesture.

The Second Vatican Council put the endeavors of all Christians for a single visible church into the closest relationship with the mission of the church to the world. Already in the introduction to the Decree on the Ecumenical movement we find a phrase that is almost identical with the theme you have chosen for this Assembly. In this introduction it is said that the church is *ad mundum universum missa*, "sent to the whole world", and that it should therefore be one if it is able to fulfil this mission.

In passing on to my theme, I may perhaps be permitted to assume that you do not expect me to do anything other than put forward some thoughts in connection with your principal theme as seen from the point of view of the Roman Catholic Church. I want to do this in all modesty and in the spirit of Paul's famous words in his letter to the Romans: in this way I would like to ensure that "we may be mutually encouraged by each other's faith, both yours and mine" (Rom. 1:12). Naturally, such considerations drawn from our faith will also throw some indirect light on our mutual relationships and on the dialog between us which is developing in an even more fruitful manner.

I.

The *fact of faith* that the church has been *sent into the world* is surely a matter of course for us. Here one can never do enough to keep one's eyes firmly fixed on the attitude to man displayed by God himself, who so loved the world that "he gave his only Son" (John 3:16). To this we must add that God "who through Christ reconciled us to himself", afterwards through the church "gave us the ministry of reconciliation" (2 Cor. 5:18). The church, and this means all of us, therefore bears a great responsibility for the world. The church, in the widest and most profound sense of the word, must be one with the world. The Pastoral Constitution on the Church in the Modern World issued by the Second Vatican Council, repeatedly stressed this solidarity: "Indeed, nothing genuinely human fails to raise an echo in their (the followers of Christ) hearts. For theirs is a community composed of men . . . this community realizes that it is truly and intimately linked with mankind and its history." (para. 1.)[1]

But, if I am not mistaken, the accent of your principal theme does not lie so much on the idea of universalism as it does on the thought that the church has been sent into the world of today, the world just as it is and, even more so, to man in the world of today. Man, as a result of his inner life rises above the totality of things. But at the same time he also belongs to the material world by virtue of his being embodied. Has the church understood this dignity of man in the concrete, has it recognized it, and has it served man in his dignity?

The dignity of man is particularly characterized by his freedom. This essential element of his dignity is considered by modern man as the real characteristic of the human person (Vatican II, *De Libertate Religiosa*, para. 1; *Gaudium et Spes*, paras. 12-22, particularly 17).

The dignity of man and his freedom concern both the bodily and the spiritual dimension, since these are inseparably linked in his person.

The decisive question for our purposes is this: What, in the concrete, is the nature of the mission of the church to such a world today?

The church has not been sent into the world with empty hands, but is rather the carrier of Christ's gospel. The priority of the gospel is given particular expression in this Assembly by the theme of the first section which is "Sent with the Gospel". The Second Vatican Council saw fit to supplement the previously quoted phrase *ad universum mundum missa*, "sent to the whole world" with the words, *ut mundus ad Evangelium convertatur*, "so that the world may become converted to the gospel". Are the Catholic Church and the Lutheran World Federation trying to understand their mission in this manner by basing themselves on the same source? 450 years ago, our forefathers thought that

---
[1] All translations of Vatican documents referred to in the text are those of the lecturer.

they had to separate in the name of the true gospel. Today we believe and hope to be able to overcome this separation (which, even at the time of its origin, was not regarded as intended, but which was merely accepted by both sides as unavoidable) in the name of the true gospel.

When we talk about the church and its mission, we are very prone to the danger of confining our discussion to abstract terms. Are we not ourselves the church? How does a Christian—and let us remember that the church lives in each individual Christian—conceive his mission? Let us listen to the answer given by the Apostle Paul, "a servant of Jesus Christ . . . set apart for the gospel of God" (Rom. 1:1). It seems to me that his answer can be traced back to the two fundamental principles. The first of these principles is to be found in his famous saying: "For though I am free from all men, I have made myself a slave to all . . . I have become all things to all men, that I might by all means save some" (1 Cor. 9:19-22).

The second principle, as well as the attitude that corresponds to it, is expressed by Paul time and time again and also in many different forms. An example is to be found in the phrase which defines the theme of the letter to the Romans: "For I am not ashamed of the gospel: it is the power of God for salvation to every one who has faith." (Rom. 1:16). Again, we find it in the following phrase: "For Jews demand signs and Greeks seek wisdom, but we preach Christ cruci- fied, a stumbling block to Jews and folly to Gentiles, but to those who are called, both Jews and Greeks, Christ the power of God and the wisdom of God" (1 Cor. 1:22-25). Both attitudes—the service of man pushed to the extreme and the courageous recognition of the folly of the cross—are thus fully justified and form an essential part of the attitude of the church vis-à-vis the world.

A first point at which the church can and should become "all things" for modern man concerns the whole field of work for the recognition of the dignity of man, for the freedom of man, for social justice, for peace. The world not only hopes, it expects the church to say the word of the gospel about these problems: in this respect the world is today extraordinarily frank and open in its relations to the church. The gospel is directed toward the whole of humanity and there- fore also to the whole of the world. But this universal orientation of the gospel also entails the secular responsibility of the church.

The Second Vatican Council made a recommendation to all Christians that the particular aim of their collaboration should be: "cooperation in the correct evalu- ation of the dignity of the human person, in the promotion of peace, in the application of gospel sociology, in securing the advance of the sciences and the arts in a Christian spirit, in the provision of every kind of cure for the troubles of our day—famine, disasters, illiteracy, want, housing shortage, inequal- ity in the distribution of food. (*De Oecumenismo*, para. 12).

The Lutheran-Catholic Study Commission, "Gospel and Church", in turn, very quickly came to recognize that for a true understanding of the gospel there is necessary not only reflection about the church, but equally reflection about the world. It therefore felt itself obliged, somewhat beyond its original program, to dedicate a whole session to the subject "Gospel and World".

At the beginning of my remarks I stressed the fact that freedom was the hallmark of the dignity of the human person. In this connection I would like to make one more quotation from a Council text: "Only in freedom can man direct himself toward goodness. Our contemporaries make much of this freedom and pursue it eagerly; and rightly so, to be sure" (*Gaudium et Spes,* para. 17). The Declaration on Religious Freedom returns to this matter in greater detail: "A sense of the dignity of the human person has been impressing itself more and more deeply on the consciousness of contemporary man. And the demand is increasingly made that men should act on their own judgment, enjoying and making use of a responsible freedom, not driven by coercion but motivated by a sense of duty. The demand is also made that constitutional limits should be set to the powers of government, in order that there may be no encroachment on the rightful freedom of the person and of associations." (*Dignitatis humanae,* para. 1).

If modern man is to develop in freedom, then he must also have a right to education in order to ensure that he will be freed from the burden of illiteracy; he further has a right to the recognition of his human dignity and to be given the possibility of developing this dignity within human society, all this quite irrespective of his race or his nationality; he also has the right to be liberated from all sub-human forms of life that prostrate him, including poverty, lack of housing, etc. Every individual human being, however small and insignificant, has a right to expect that the mighty in human society will develop a world economy that will free him from famine and epidemics: he has a right for the state to be based on a juridical order that recognizes his dignity and will protect his human rights, particularly through the courts, even when he is in prison; further, he has a right to expect that the great powers will free him from the threat of war and will create an order of peace. (A program for this service to man is described in the encyclical *Populorum Progressio.*) The freedom of man, inasmuch as it is a personal and fundamental characteristic of his nature that also governs his inter-personal relationships with his fellow men, can only exist in an order of society that recognizes and guarantees these rights.

But can this freedom really be understood in a purely human or this-worldly sense? Luther, in his text entitled "About the Freedom of Christian Man", pointed to the gospel as the origin of freedom. It seems to me essential that we should penetrate to these depths of the Christian faith if we want to obtain a proper understanding of the freedom of man and the mission of the church to the world.

Let us now assume that we have done everything possible in the secular domain, let us even assume—and this surely is not possible—that we have solved all the tasks which have been presented in this field. Would we then have done justice to the mission of the church in the world? Not by any means. We would then still find ourselves at the very beginning of the real and most profound mission, the mission to bring to the world the gospel of Christ and therefore Christ himself. The fulfilment of this task is called for by the very need to help the dignity of man to attain its full development. Secularism tends towards imprisoning man in a closed world. But such a restriction would endanger or even destroy true and complete human dignity, the integral vocation of man (cf. *Populorum Progressio*, para. 42).

For the very reason that the church has been sent into the world, it must also be the conscience of mankind: it must not identify itself with the "world", but rather must be the salt of the earth and the light that illuminates man's way through this world.

The task that I have sketched with these words is of fundamental importance. It therefore seems to me to be appropriate to illustrate it in greater detail on the basis of the gospel.

1) The dignity of man attains its highest perfection when man recognizes God and adores him. "Authentic freedom is an exceptional sign of the divine image within man" *(Gaudium et Spes,* para. 17). God alone is supremely free. The Christian does not know him as an Unknown God, but as his Father. A world in which God is not recognized and adored, by virtue of this very reason, becomes uninhabitable for man. This arises quite unmistakably from the broad line of the messianic prophecies about the coming of the kingdom of God, and this quite irrespective of the exact determination of the messianic character and the precise interpretation of the individual passages. In the last resort, justice and peace are due to the fact that the earth is "full of the knowledge of the Lord", "as the waters cover the sea" (Isaiah 11:9). Here we also find the reason why the pacification of man extends over the whole of creation (cf. Isaiah 11:6 f).

Christ himself speaks in the same sense when he pronounces his high-priestly prayer about eternal life and says: "And this is eternal life, that they know Thee the only true God, and Jesus Christ whom Thou hast sent" (John 17:3).

2) However, the way and even the necessary prerequisite for this dedication of man to God, and therefore for the adoration of God in spirit and truth (cf. John 4:24), is the reconciliation between God and man brought about by Jesus Christ (cf. Isaiah 53:11; Matt. 20:28; Mark 10:45; Romans 5:6, 8, 10).

3) But the liberation of man through the action of Jesus Christ is most closely connected with the reconciliation with God. We cannot understand the concept of the freedom brought to us by Jesus Christ in a purely this-worldly manner,

we cannot therefore allow it to become "secularized". On the basis of the New Testament it is simply not admissible to think only of the social liberation of man in this connection. Through Jesus Christ the Heavenly Father has "delivered us from the dominion of darkness" (Col. 1:13). The inner freedom of the children of God is also the reason and the origin of social justice and freedom. This does not mean that we must sacralize the worldly or the "secular". It only means that we must correctly see the connection between the holy and the worldly. Otherwise, how could one say that the church has been sent into the world?

4) But the liberation brought about by Jesus Christ is not just a negative one, it does not just consist of liberation from the dominion of darkness. In the text from the letter to the Colossians which I have just quoted, Paul adds immediately afterwards that the Father "has transferred us to the kingdom of his beloved Son" (Col. 1:13). But precisely because we have become sons of God in Jesus Christ and thus belong to his family, this world cannot be our permanent and final resting place (cf. Letter to the Hebrews, 13, 14).

Moreover, the specifically Christian vision of this age is also determined on the basis of this conception. According to the well known arguments of the letter to the Romans, the whole of creation in a certain sense feels its own impermanence. This feeling then becomes associated with the general longing for a final liberation of man and the whole of creation, the liberation from the slavery of impermanence and death (cf. Romans 8:19-22).

We have already received the first fruits of the Spirit and with that the pledge of final liberation. It is because of this that the glorified Lord "will change our lowly body to be like his glorious body, by the power which enables him even to subject all things to himself" (Phil. 3:21).

5) With what I have said up to now, it would seem that I have listed the principal points of the gospel that cause particular difficulty for the secularized world of today: the meaning and the importance of the recognition of God, redemption and the reconciliation with God, the deeper meaning of the freedom that has been given us through Jesus Christ, the correct appreciation of the present epoch.

The stressing of these points must not be misunderstood in the sense that we underestimate this world or the work of building it up. Quite the contrary. This particular manner of the revelation of God constitutes the very basis for the hopeful faith with which the Christian dedicates himself to the improvement of this world. It is this very revelation that gives us the firm conviction that it will be possible to construct a better world. The "eschaton" is the true and perfect reality. But the future world does not fall ready-made from heaven, but rather has to be prepared in this age (cf. *Gaudium et Spes,* para. 39). On the basis of these principles, earthly progress must be directed towards the well-being of man; if this is not done, earthly progress could also become demoniacal. The poor and the weak of our times already feel the threat that stems from this.

Can our two traditions help each other, can they allow themselves to be helped in their joint service for the gospel with a view to the liberation of man, the liberation of the world? Such mutual help would surely be a very promising way to the re-creation of our lost unity. After all, this service would spur us to tackle our important worldly tasks in a more conscious manner and would thereby free us from quite a few historical controversies. Even this indirect manner of a joint service with a view to doing justice to the problems and the challenges of the world of today could help Christians and their respective ecclesial traditions to come closer to each other.

II.

Having thus expressed my thoughts as regards the general theme of this Assembly, I would now like to speak to you about Catholic-Lutheran relations in the present and in the future. First of all, may I crave your indulgence to talk very briefly about the events of the last few years, even if in so doing I may have to refer to matters that are perhaps widely known.

The Lutheran Churches made a very substantial contribution towards the better ecumenical understanding that has come into being in many places both during and after the Second World War. It is therefore quite readily understandable that the Lutheran World Federation, founded in 1947, had an ecumenical orientation right from the start, so much so that its original constitution defines one of its aims as "promoting Lutheran participation in ecumenical movements". The Assemblies of your Federation have also dealt rather fully with parts of the ecumenical problem. The greatest intensification of the ecumenical movement, as is well known, occurred at your last Assembly in Helsinki, where it was formulated that the tasks of the Lutheran World Federation included "promoting the interest and participation of Lutheran Churches in ecumenical movements and strengthening their responsibility for such movements". That these were not empty words was clearly shown by the creation of the "Lutheran Foundation for Ecumenical Research" and the subsequent setting up of the research institute in Strasbourg.

For historically understandable reasons, wide circles of the world Lutheran movement regarded the Roman Catholic Church as a particularly important interlocutor. It was not therefore surprising that the Lutheran World Federation should have followed the Second Vatican Council with particular care—three study volumes bear eloquent witness to this—and that it was the first confessional association on a world scale to begin an official dialog with Rome, a development that could not yet be foreseen at the time of your last Assembly. The Lutheran World Federation and the Roman Catholic Church have now been in dialog for the last six years. The study commission "The Gospel and the Church" will terminate its labors in the near future, presumably some time next year. Moreover, the time is not far off when both sides will be required to give a report rendering account of their work. After several years of informative discussions, where do we today see the fundamental things we have in common and where do we see the unbridgeable differences? Has it been found possible to enlarge the common basis? Connected with all this there is a possibly even more important question: Has the dialog proceeded in a continuous manner? In 1965, on the occasion of the first session of the Catholic-Lutheran working group in Strasbourg, Dr. Kurt Schmidt-Clausen,[1] who was at that time General Secretary of the Lutheran World Federation, said that one would have to develop a "strategy of the dialog", in order to ensure that the Lutheran-Catholic dialog would not once again degenerate into a theological battle of wits and that the dialog would be conducted with each other and not against each other. He said that the premises for a dialog that really deserved this name lay in the planning of a discussion that was real, all-embracing and thorough, a discussion that did not sin against truth. A discussion in which regional groups could meaningfully participate and which at the same time was so designed that the overall dialog would be promoted in all its ramifications, a discussion that would ensure appropriate treatment of all the central points of the dissent, but without neglecting problems that were regarded as (or seemed to be) marginal . . . The fateful temptation of putting easy solutions or even ecclesio-political manipulations into the place of a factual treatment of the difficult phases of the dialog, he said, had to be firmly resisted.

Today, six years after the beginning of the Lutheran-Catholic dialog, it will be a good thing if we take note of the dangers that were pointed out at the very start and if we set the rails in such a way that both traditions will really continue to face the risks of the dialog. If we do not do this, there could well be a disillusion that might nullify the promising beginnings and Lutheran-Catholic relations could then become more difficult than they were at the beginning of the dialog.

The links between the dialog that is being carried on at an international level and the regional or local discussion groups have not yet been made in practice or, at least, not sufficiently. In the first place, it is quite clear today that dialog in the form of scientific-theological discussions, however necessary it may be, is not by itself sufficient. Christ is the Way, the Truth and the Life. Christians and pastors, to whom Christ has entrusted the task of governing the church, in truth and for the sake of truth, will also have to seek joint roads and a joint life. Even the theological discussion itself should provide inspiration in this direction. And everything I have previously said in connection with the theme of this Assembly also points in this direction.

In spite of all the prospects for the future, the Catholic-Lutheran dialog must

---

[1] Dr Kurt Schmidt-Clausen in his address entitled "Content, shape and scope of the possible contacts and cooperation between the Roman Catholic Church and the Lutheran World Federation", Minutes of the first consulative session of the joint Roman Catholic and Lutheran Evangelical working group, Strasbourg, August 25-27, 1965.

always look back to the sixteenth century. There can be no doubt that many of the controversies of that time appear in a new light today. Many questions, which at that time stood at the very center of controversy, have today been partly pushed towards the periphery and are now barely felt as controversial. An example of this is to be found in the doctrine of justification as such. It has been shown that extensive misunderstandings came into play on both sides and that these made a factual discussion impossible. The ecumenical dialog has now been going on for some decades and the situation has been substantially improved.

In spite of this positive development, however, it would not be correct to say that all the questions that have divided us ever since the sixteenth century have already resolved themselves of their own accord. I am now thinking about the central doctrines of the church, and more particularly of the questions regarding the ministry, the authority, the infallibility, the position of the Pope, and the general questions of the ecclesial structures. I am also thinking of the position occupied by the Virgin Mary, Mother of God, in the mystery of Christ and the church. In these matters the confessional situation has not always become easier since the times of the Reformation, indeed, in some matters the contrasts have even become sharpened. If today we cannot yet see the outlines of a real rapprochement in all these questions, then we must once again bear in mind that the ecumenical task will be solved first and foremost by the Spirit of God, because it far transcends our human endeavors. Only as a result of God's action can unity come into being.

III.

Martin Luther

As I have already said, the Lutheran-Catholic dialog cannot overlook the controversies of the sixteenth century. This is no less true as regards the person and the work of Martin Luther from whom your world wide family takes it name.

I want to follow in Cardinal Bea's footsteps and stress that what I am about to say is not intended to distribute the blame for this unfortunate division; we should rather seek together for ways and means to re-create our lost unity.[2] Who would not agree that a correct appreciation of the person and the work of Martin Luther forms part of this endeavor on our part?[3]

----

[2] Letter written by Cardinal Bea to President Schiotz in 1967 on the occasion of the 20th anniversary of the foundation of the Lutheran World Federation and the 450th anniversary of the Reformation.

[3] In this connection see also Yves M.-J Congar who wrote the following in an article entitled "Expérience et conversion oecuméniques. Témoignage", published in Chrétiens en dialogue, (Paris: Les Editions du Cerf, 1964), pp. 123-139. "Je sais, hélas!, que Luther a encore aujourd'hui un très mauvais renom chez les catholiques, sauf peut-être en Allemagne. Je saia qu'il y a en lui de quoit justifier ce renom. Je sais aussi qu'on ne rend justice, ainsi, ni à son intention foncière, ni même à sa pensée religieuse. Je sais enfin quote rien de tout sérieux ne sera fait de notre part vers le protéstantisme, tant qu'on naura pas accompli la dèmarche de comprendre vraiment Luther et de lui rendre historiquement justice, au lieu de simplement le condamner. Pour cette conviction, qui est menne, je serais prêt à donner joyeusement ma vie.", p. 126.

The person of Martin Luther has not always been correctly appreciated by the Catholic side in the course of centuries and his theology has not always been correctly presented. This has served neither truth nor love, and therefore it has not served the unity that we are endeavoring to establish between yourselves and the Catholic Church. On the other hand, we may note with pleasure that the last few decades have seen the growth of a scientifically more correct understanding of the Reformation among Catholic scholars and, consequently, also of the figure of Martin Luther and his theology.

If today, 450 years after the decisive year of 1520, I speak to you in this manner, it is because I am fully conscious of the many inhibitions that still exist between you and us as a result of the forceful personality of Martin Luther and his work. These inhibitions have always led the Catholic Church to maintain a certain reserve. But love drives out the fear of being misunderstood, and years of dialog have removed many of the misunderstandings.

Who, and now I refer to ourselves, would still deny that Martin Luther was a deeply religious person who with honesty and dedication sought for the message of the gospel? Who would deny that in spite of the fact that he fought against the Roman Catholic Church and the Apostolic See—and for the sake of truth one must not remain silent about this—he retained a considerable part of the old Catholic faith? Indeed, is it not true that the Second Vatican Council has even implemented requests which were first expressed by Martin Luther, among others, and as a result of which many aspects of Christian faith and life now find better expression than they did before? To be able to say this in spite of all the differences is a reason for great joy and much hope.

In a manner that was quite extraordinary for the times in which he lived, Martin Luther made the Bible the starting point of theology and Christian life. Ever since that time, the Bible has been treated as a special treasure in all your churches and has been studied with the greatest zeal. The Second Vatican Council, for its own part, has inserted the Holy Scriptures, which have always been a great treasure of the Catholic Church as profoundly into the life of the church and its members that the Bible becomes richer and more fruitful for them. In this spirit the Council goes on to say: "Nevertheless, in the dialogue, the sacred utterances are surpassing instruments in the powerful hand of God for winning the unity which the Savior offers to all men" (*De Oecumenismo*, para. 21).

But there is *one* word that recurs time and time again in Martin Luther: the lofty word "faith". Luther profoundly realized its value and many people in your churches, indeed far beyond your churches, have since learned to live through it. Even though there would seem to be a certain onesidedness in this matter, and one might properly conclude this in view of the excessive emphasis that Martin Luther's speeches place on it, the joint research of Catholic and Evangelical theologians has nevertheless shown that the word "faith" in Luther's sense does by no means intend to exclude either works, or love, or hope. One may well say, and with much good reason, that Luther's concept of faith, when taken in its full meaning, might not really mean anything other than what we designate by the word love in the Catholic Church.

It is not necessary, indeed it would not be possible, to present here the central points of Luther's theology. A great deal would have to be said about his theology of the cross, his christology, the stress he placed on the divinity of Christ, a matter in which today we feel particularly close to him. On the other hand, many scholars, both Catholics and Protestants, have pointed out that it is very difficult to re-state Luther's thoughts in a manner that is precise, exhaustive and, above all, evenly balanced: in short it is difficult to state his thinking in such a way as to do justice to the multiplicity of his formulations which, after all, he never really developed in a systematic manner.

It is a consolation for me to think that we also share the same sentiments if in these joint reflections I prefer to say nothing about certain particularly sharp attacks that Martin Luther made against the Roman Pontiff; they sadden my heart and I feel sure that you, too, regard them as a burden.

At a meeting which has set its theme as "The Mission to the World", it is undoubtedly a good thing to recall to mind a man for whom the doctrine of justification was the "articulus stantis et cadentis Ecclesiae". In this we could all learn from him that God must always remain the Lord, and that our most important human answer must always remain absolute confidence in God and our adoration of him.

IV.

Prospectives of greater communion

May I be permitted to conclude my remarks by mentioning some prospectives for the immediate future. What concrete steps directed towards a closer communion are conceivable during the years to come? The course hitherto taken by our discussions, by even the Second Vatican Council itself, can give us some hint in this matter. Although the Vatican Council frequently spoke about dialog, it never gave any concrete suggestion as to what should be the principal subject of this dialog. There is just one exception to this general rule: in connection with its statement about baptism and the Eucharist, the Council has this to say: "For this reason, the teaching on the Lord's Supper, the other sacraments, the worship and ministry of the Church should constitute the subject matter of the dialogue" (Unitatis Redintegratio, para. 22). Further on, the same Document also speaks of the ecumenical dialog regarding the application of the gospel to moral questions in the world (Unitatis Redintegratio, para. 23). With this, ever since 1964, a certain direction has been given which during the subsequent years of the Lutheran-Catholic dialog has proved to be both central and essential. In fact, the discussion developed in such a way that problems regarding the ministry and the Eucharist have come more and more towards the center of reflection in both the international dialog and in the national ones. All results leading to greater agreement in these matters will make an essential contribution to bringing us nearer to the moment when we will be able to celebrate the unity-creating Supper of our Lord together.

I would also like to underline the importance of joint witness: all those who have received the faith in Jesus Christ are called upon within the limits of their possibilities, to bear joint witness to this faith. This has always been of fundamental importance. In a secularized world, however, it is of incomparably greater importance. Only personal witness will ensure that the message of the gospel reaches the world in a vital way. Only in this way can we succeed in making the glad tidings enter into the life of secularized society and in turning the gospel into the leaven of the world.

By virtue of its mission in the world, the church today finds itself face to face with new and difficult tasks. The faith in Jesus Christ gives us the strength to tackle them (cf. 1 John 5:4). If together we can give form to the Christian mission in the world, then we will also find in this mission a forceful impetus toward our full unity in Christ. This unity is in the first place a value in itself, because it represents a participation in the unity of Christ with the Father (cf. John 17:21 f) and because it is desired as such by Christ and was requested by him from the Father. On the other hand, unity and therefore also our endeavor for its realization, stands in the service of the mission of the church, the very unity for which Christ prayed in his high-priestly prayer so that the world might believe that he has been sent by the Father (cf. John 17:21).

Let us never cease to practice truth in love (cf. Eph. 4:15) so that we may both come closer to each other, driven by our faith in and our love for our one Lord Jesus Christ.

Sent With the Gospel

Introduction

(1) This report is based on intensive discussions which have taken place at this Assembly under the section theme, "Sent with the Gospel". These discussions are especially important in view of the fact that world Lutheranism is devoting major attention to the mission of the church in the modern world.

(2) The difficulties which were encountered in the discussion were primarily due to the lack of time required to reach a consensus in an Assembly involving global participation. We wish it had been possible to share our experiences and ideas more fully.

(3) In the midst of the wide diversity of issues raised and the many attitudes which we take towards them, we sense nevertheless that we are one in faith and love, and we long to share this not only with one another but with the whole world. We believe that just as Jesus Christ was sent by God into the world to redeem the world, so we have been sent by Jesus joyfully to proclaim the gospel in love and with justice.

(4) Many of us have entered into the discussions in the hope that a rather broad consensus would be reached. It has been necessary for us first to face our differences and to recognize that to strive for a false consensus would be wrong. We must recognize that the differences among us may be a gift of the Holy Spirit. A frank recognition of these differences may eventually become an enrichment of our life together. It may also lead us into a deeper understanding of the nature of our missionary existence and of the way in which we can communicate the good news concerning God's free gift of grace to the world today.

I. *The Power of the Gospel in Mission*

(5) The power of the gospel is evident to us when we, both individually and as a church, are confronted with our own sin, impossible to repair; in our confrontation with our own death, impossible to avoid; and in our confrontation with the total need of mankind, impossible to neglect.

(6) Jesus Christ who himself is the gospel, has descended to our anguish. To accept the fact that I am a sinner, and that I, in spite of that, receive a new life and am called to a new service, is to have forgiveness of sins through the cross of Christ. To accept the fact that death is at the door before us, but that we, in spite of this fact, go from life to life, is to receive

the resurrection of the dead through the resurrection of Christ. Through this same gospel we are set free to fulfill the will of God. To accept the fact that the needs of our neighbors direct our deeds and actions in our service to the Lord, obligates us to a constant review of our ministry to the world. The service which we thereby receive from Christ as members of his body, gives us the power to fulfill this ministry, even in a hostile environment.

(7) In these confrontations the Holy Spirit also today through the gospel gives us power to live and serve and celebrate. This power we cannot receive without being sent to the world, and in our going out to witness and serve we are receiving this power according to our needs.

II. *The Charismatic Congregation*

(8) In connection with the problem of mission and power the charismatic congregation was also discussed on the basis of the question: What is the place of charismata in our congregations and how do we acknowledge and put to use the gifts of the Spirit?

(9) The following points were mentioned:

a) How does our church meet the misunderstanding that the pastor has a monopoly on spiritual gifts and suppresses the spiritual gift of all the baptized by his leading role? It was repeatedly asked what the special gifts and tasks of the pastor are, and also what the special gifts and tasks of all the members of the congregation are. Rightly understood, the Lutheran Church must be anticlerical. Against the background of the tasks, God shows what the gifts are. To articulate and educate these gifts is a responsibility which rests not only with the leaders of the congregations. The upbuilding is a mutual process.

b) The charisma is not only given to the individual but to every congregation. Therefore, it must ask itself what charisma it has for the other congregations and for its surroundings. The more intensively we live our charismata as a congregation, the farther we reach out in the world. This is particularly the experience of the congregations in states built on a very strong political ideology.

c) Is not theology too a charisma? If that is so, then every church can learn from the theology of other churches. For the younger churches the question is, however, how they can develop their own theology in relation to European churches without being fettered, as they must find their own language for their own people.

III. *Structure of the Church in Mission*

(10) All subsection discussions were affected by the problems of structures

relating to the task of mission in the whole world. It was generally agreed that the local congregation as a unit of the church should be made more effective than at present for witness and service in its own environment. Churches should be helped to reconsider their structures to facilitate a functional witness by the congregation, by individuals, by small functional groups, and by the total congregation (e.g., an urban congregation, a congregation in the slums, a student congregation, etc.).

(11) A stronger international fellowship of the churches will mutually enrich all churches in the world, but this is possible only if churches and their organizations for mission are not too anxious for self-preservation, but will open themselves. Some suggested a fuller international pooling of church funds and personnel for exchange throughout the world. The logistics of such an enterprise have to be worked out carefully. The spontaneity of God's mission should be encouraged, recognizing that it may lead to something quite new.

IV. *The Gospel and Diaconial Development*

(12) From the beginning the Christian commission has included both proclamation and service, because our Lord was concerned for every aspect of life. The gospel is expressed in words and is illuminated by acts of love. God's revelation in Christ and the resources of his created world are given equally for all men. The Christian is sent to share with others both the material and the spiritual gifts with which he has been entrusted.

(13) In the modern world, when the physical distress of a great part of mankind has become a scandal to our consciences and a barrier to human fellowship, Christians are more aware than ever of the joyful obligation to meet physical as well as spiritual need, not only through deeds of individual love, but also by participating corporately in the alleviation of distress and in the development process.

(14) On the question of the relation of such efforts of serving the word (which are a form of witness) to the proclamation of the kingdom of the crucified and risen Christ (which is a supreme act of service to men), there was no full agreement in the section. Must, for example, the act always be accompanied by the word, if it is to be more than humanitarian altruism? Does the spoken word lack reality, if unaccompanied by Christian self-sacrifice in deed?

(15) On this we seemed to be agreed: that full humanness is not possible without knowledge of God's redemption, and that the act of service in Jesus' name is an end in itself, not to be seen as a means for another purpose.

RECOMMENDATIONS OF SECTION I, INCLUDING ACTIONS
TAKEN BY THE ASSEMBLY

Recommendations Regarding LWF Structure

1. Alarmed and concerned over the omission of the word mission, and by implication the concept of mission, from the proposed new structure, we *recommend* that the name of the proposed "Commission on Church Cooperation" be changed to "Commission on Church Cooperation in World Mission".

   This resolution was not adopted by the Assembly (see item 34 of the minutes, p. 143 f).

2. Alert to avoid the danger of a separation between witness and service in the life of the LWF and its member churches, and fearing an institutional separation between Church Cooperation and World Service, we *recommend* that the Executive Committee take firm steps to assure an organizational relationship between these two commissions which incorporates the proper theological understanding of the relationship between witness and service.

   On the recommendation of the PRC, the Assembly voted that this recommendation be transmitted to the new Executive Committee, taking into account that all commissions of the LWF should be in cooperation with one another (see item 33b of the minutes, p. 142).

3. We strongly *recommend* that the whole working process of the LWF Assembly be reviewed, and that in any case for future assemblies working groups of the size of the present unwieldy subsections should not be set up, but that smaller groups should be established and given more time and sessions and that the issues be developed according to modern pedagogical principles, so as to permit meaningful dialog across member church, nationality, regional, and generation groupings.

   On the recommendation of the PRC the Assembly decided to defer action until further recommendations from other sources regarding the same issue are on hand (see item 61 of the minutes, p. 159).

Recommendations Regarding LWF Studies

1. Realizing the need to activate congregations toward mission, and to help them to recognize their responsibilities and potential for effective witness and service, we *recommend* that the Commission on Studies encourage the member churches to undertake practical case studies of congregations or groups of congregations to explore and to share more widely in

a variety of languages the nature and direction of their Christian witness and service in their given situation.

2. Aware of questions raised about the value of small groups, we *recommend* that the Commission on Studies undertake an interdisciplinary study of the usefulness of small groups, and that it report its findings for use by congregations, theological faculties, and administrators.

3. We *recommend* that the Commission on Studies in cooperation with the WCC and other organizations, research the possibilities and suggest guidelines to help members of the participating churches to begin, or to carry on, dialogs with atheists and with men of other faiths, and that it foster an exchange of information between groups participating in such studies.

4. We *recommend* that the Commission on Studies investigate the relationship between the preaching of the church and its word spoken publicly in such means as study documents and appeals to public representatives in the fields of politics and economics. This also should involve a clarification of the issue of the "political sermon".

On the recommendation of the PRC, it was voted to transmit all four recommendations to the new Executive Committee without prejudice (see item 33b of the minutes, p. 142).

Recommendations Regarding Social Responsibility

1. We recommend for receipt and transmittal to the member churches, for their consideration and such action as they deem appropriate the following resolution:

WHEREAS, all Christians must provide an active witness in society, and not to do so is to leave unfulfilled a Christian duty and privilege, and

WHEREAS, a church cannot exist in a vacuum, separated from the society in which it is sent for witness and service, therefore be it

RESOLVED, that the LWF urge all its member churches to work to sensitize their congregations to the cultural, political, social, and economic situations in which they live, as well as to the Christian obligations of these congregations within these situations, and be it further

RESOLVED, that the LWF take the necessary steps to encourage those in positions of leadership, as well as those preparing for such positions, to become qualified to contribute to the task of bringing the Christian witness to the societies in which they live, stressing the Christian social responsibility demanded by a living Christian faith.

2. We *recommend* for receipt and transmittal to the member churches for their consideration and appropriate action the following resolution:

RESOLVED, that the LWF urge its member churches as organized religious institutions to seek to go to the roots of social injustice and inequities by using their resources for research and analysis of social problems, to become involved in studies on these issues which seek to develop a vision of goals for action and means to these desired goals, and to use their corporate influence toward the ends of justice and equity.

On the recommendation of the PRC, the Assembly voted that these two recommendations be received and transmitted to the member churches for their consideration and appropriate action (see item 33b of the minutes. p. 142).

SECTION II REPORT

Ecumenical Commitment

Introduction

(1) The task of Section II has been that of reflecting on the ecumenical commitment of the LWF and its member churches. We have discussed a variety of topics: the urgency, necessity, and some of the dimensions of Christian unity; the problem of inner-Lutheran fellowship; the role of the LWF in the ecumenical movement; some new frontiers in Lutheran relations to Baptist and Methodist churches, Pentecostalism and independent Christian movements; and a new trend in ecumenical experimentation, the so-called secular ecumenism. Because of the range of problems dealt with by our section, and the limitations of time imposed on us, we have not attempted to bring the contributions of the separate groups into a unified report, but present them as the results of the discussions in the subsections together with their recommendations for the future work of the LWF.

(2) The study document, "More Than Unity of Churches", prepared by the Commission on Theology of the LWF and published in *Lutheran World* (Vol. XVII, No. 1, 1970), provided the basis for the discussions of the section and should be consulted as the background of these discussions. The document makes no pretence to be an exhaustive treatment of the subject of unity, but does seek to introduce some new elements into the exchange of views within the Federation.

Subsection 1: The Unity of the Church

I. *The Urgency of Christian Unity*

(3) Dissatisfaction concerning divisions within the churches, and movements toward unity of Christians are both stronger today than ever before. There are many impulses at work in this area; we would stress three that seem to us to be especially important.

First, the yearning for that unity of the church which is given in Christ and without which the church cannot effectively carry out her mission or know any peace in a separated existence.

Second, the work of the Holy Spirit in renewing the church. This renewal is not confined to any one tradition, or brought about by the resources of a particular confessional group, but demands the total riches of the church of Christ, since a divided church is not really equipped for the service of reconciliation in a broken world.

Third, the challenge by a world which becomes increasingly one world through technological developments and at the same time is frightened by what it has created and looks anxiously for purpose and meaning in human life and history.

(4) Amid these changes we can perceive the work of the triune God who has taken worldly power away from us as churches and called us again to our proper role as servants. The churches are distressed by the loss of this worldly power and prestige, but we can now see that such power not only falsified our function in the world but nourished self-satisfaction and pride which helped keep us apart from other churches.

II. *What Is Necessary for Christian Unity?*

(5) That which is necessary for the unity of the church is identical to that which constitutes the church: Jesus Christ, present in the gospel, proclaimed through word and sacrament, and received by faith. This encounter with the living Christ occurs whenever through sermon, baptism, and eucharist, in accordance with the witness of the Scriptures, men receive the assurance that they are justified through grace alone. In all congregations where this proclamation of Christ takes place effectually, the prerequisite for church fellowship is already present. The differences which still exist in the interpretation and application of the gospel in doctrine and orders are not valid reasons for dividing the churches from one another. This conviction is the unexpended ecumenical capital of the Lutheran tradition. It is part of the Reformation doctrine of the church (CA VII), but its consequences have not been drawn either within the Lutheran family or in our relationships with other churches.

(6) The proclamation of the gospel thus finds its unity in the fact that it speaks of nothing other than Jesus Christ the one Lord and Reconciler. One baptism, one eucharist, one Holy Scripture point to this unity. But this one source of unity is interpreted in the New Testament in a great variety of vocabularies and thought patterns, which cannot be reduced to theological uniformity, but testify to the richness and diversity by which the early disciples interpreted the mission, death, and resurrection of Jesus Christ. In our search for unity today, we must not insist upon uniformity in theological formulations and in practice but use the variations rooted in the Scriptures to help bring together divided groups of people in the world into "one body with many members".

III. *Unity in Faith and in Service*

(7) The response of Christians to the word of forgiveness includes the doxology of worship and proclamation, of theological reflection, and of service in and for the world. The service of Christ which the church carries out in this world compels us to move forward on the path toward unity. Christians of all confessions and in all parts of the world recognize this today as a result of intensive listening to the message of the gospel. It would be a dangerous misunderstanding of the meaning of unity to confine the search for unity either to areas of common serving or to questions of theology and faith. Unity in serving cannot be separated from unity in faith, for the common life in Christ includes both growth in serving men in the world and in a deepening understanding of the mystery of God in Christ.

Subsection 2A: Fellowship among Lutheran Churches and Union Negotiations

I. *Fellowship among Lutheran Churches*

(8) Christians and churches of the Lutheran confession can only speak credibly of Christian unity if they make an effort to realize unity among themselves.

(9) The situation in which the church bears its witness must be taken seriously as a determining factor in the question of fellowship among churches of the Lutheran confession. In the light of the New Testament as well as the Augsburg Confession, the mandate and mission of the church appear as primary, and the problem of the unity of the church must be understood from that viewpoint.

(10) The priority of mission has, in the present missionary and diaspora situation, again become very clear for all Lutheran churches. In such a context, the question regarding church fellowship must be asked from the standpoint of pastoral, diaconic, and missionary responsibility and urgency.

This means, first that the various Lutheran churches—especially where they are not yet in full church fellowship—should be ready to undertake pastoral, social, and diaconic tasks jointly with more vigor than heretofore. This should be seen as a promising way of learning to understand one another better and of allowing their fellowship to grow. It is a matter of finding "transitional forms" or stages of fellowship. In this sense, something like *de facto* fellowship among Lutheran churches already exists in many places, although these churches do not yet live together in full church fellowship. In this way the goal of altar and pulpit fellowship should always be kept in mind.

Second, one dare not overlook the necessity of a common understanding concerning the central questions of faith and confession. This effort which is the purpose of doctrinal discussions, must be oriented toward the mandate of proclamation. Seeking guidance from the Lutheran confessions for our proclamation and service in the present situation must do more than simply refer to the confessional statements of the Reformation fathers. Nor can our answer be found only in our response to the contemporary questions and current problems.

(11) The concern is that we together interpret the gospel anew from the viewpoint of the present context of our witness and formulate this reinterpretation. A constant criterion for this new interpretation will be its consonance with the basic intent of the Lutheran confessions, namely, the justification of the sinner through faith for the sake of Christ.

(12) Both our agreement in confession and doctrine, as well as our quest for presently viable forms of fellowship, belong together. Common confession and common doctrine are not merely the consequent fulfillment of previously existing fellowship, nor, conversely, is the existence of fellowship a consequence of having reached agreement on doctrine. Both must grow together and deepen.

(13) The emphasis on the mission aspect and on the concrete witness-context can, on the one hand, open new possibilities for Lutheran unity on the local or regional level. On the other hand, however, it can create new problems as far as the fellowship of all Lutheran churches is concerned. In this situation, too, Augustana VII can give us our correct orientation.

II. Fellowship among All Churches

(14) The question of unity among Lutheran churches cannot be solved in self-centeredness and isolation, but rather in the context of neighboring non-Lutheran churches and the universal church. For the sake of our common Christian witness and service, we must therefore be willing to listen to each other and to work toward greater fellowship. Along these lines, the

LWF has been conducting (or planning) dialogs with the Reformed churches, the Roman Catholic Church, the Anglican Communion, and the Orthodox churches for several years.

(15) The effort toward greater organizational fellowship should be closely connected with the struggle for greater fellowship in understanding the Holy Scriptures. This means a modification of the previous thesis of "formulated consensus as the prerequisite for church fellowship", but it is also a rejection of the opposing thesis of "cooperation first and then clarification of doctrinal differences".

(16) In interconfessional encounters, the Lutheran church has always seen its task as one of insisting that all churches should connect the question of unity with the question of the truth of the gospel. It has often been too self-confident in its advocacy of "pure" doctrine. This, however, does not absolve it from the responsibility of continually posing the question of truth in the search for unity.

(17) When meeting with other churches, the church of the Lutheran confession has the responsibility of bringing the message of justification in the interpretation of Holy Scripture. In so doing, it should make clear that justification is also the source from which right action proceeds.

(18) The *satis est* (CA VII) is valid not only for the relationship of Lutheran churches among themselves, but also for fellowship with the other churches. To make additional demands as a prerequisite for church fellowship is to deny the ecumenical dimension of the Reformation confession. Diversity in organizational forms and theological schools of thought does not set aside church fellowship.

(19) In doctrinal conversations with other churches, we should examine whether or not the substance of the basic articles of the Lutheran confessions could be the determining point of departure. What is necessary in the face of today's anxiety and the diaspora situation, is concentration on the fundamental questions, and not joint work on a *summa doctrinae*.

(20) Although the confessions of our fathers are helpful to us in confessing our faith today, we are responsible above all for actualizing those confessions in the face of the challenges of our times. Only if we can articulate what the confession of the Reformation means for the church's service to the world today, will it have any effect in Christendom as a whole. A purely fundamentalistic and legalistic use corresponds neither to the intention of the Lutheran confessions themselves, nor to our insight that all Christian confessional statements are historically conditioned.

III. *The Role of the Lutheran World Federation*

(21) Although the LWF is not the final expression of Lutheran fellowship, it enables churches to become more conscious of the universality of the church. They find themselves involved in a process of growth through the exchange of spiritual gifts. They receive a new attitude that challenges their self-sufficiency and opens them to new forms of common life and witness.

(22) Therefore the LWF should assume the following tasks:

a) To provide regular information on possibilities and opportunities of inner-Lutheran fellowship, as well as Lutheran ecumenical commitment.

b) To initiate and plan studies concerning the various issues relevant to the search for deeper fellowship.

c) To establish regular contacts between churches and carry out visitations.

d) To assist the churches engaged in union negotiations or interconfessional dialog.

e) To develop opportunities for a common witness and service to the world.

Subsection 2B: Our Relationship to the World Council of Churches and Our Self-Understanding as a World Confessional Family

(23) Both the LWF and the World Council of Churches are federations of churches which confess the catholicity and apostolicity of the church. This agreement includes the opportunity of closest cooperation as well as the danger of competition. Because of the similarity of purpose we have to answer the question whether the LWF and the WCC may be in each other's way. It is most important that both ecumenical bodies do not regard each other as competing organizations.

(24) It is the nature of the WCC that in its fellowship the distinct gifts of the individual churches are shared. From its beginnings and by constitutional vision the LWF was designed for service within the ecumenical movement. Lutherans are convinced that the gifts and insights of the Reformation have to be introduced into the ecumenical conversation. Together with the other world confessional families the LWF fosters international dialog, as well as the closer fellowship of the churches. In this way it contributes substantially to the general ecumenical development (e.g., Lutheran/Reformed and Lutheran/Roman Catholic relationships).

(25) On these grounds a very fruitful cooperation in many respects has already developed between the WCC and the LWF. This cooperation should be intensified in every way possible. New levels and methods of cooperation should be considered.

(26) In ecumenical dialog, as well as in its theological work within the framework of the WCC, the LWF should continue to urge the questions which were raised by the Reformation. For the extension of church fellowship beyond the Lutheran family the only prerequisite should be a basic agreement on the gospel and the sacraments according to the Scriptures (*satis est*, CA VII).

Subsection 3A: The Extension of Our Ecumenical Encounter—Baptists and Methodists

I. *General Considerations*

(27) The group felt very much handicapped in its discussion by the fact that Baptist and Methodist participants had been invited but were unable to attend because of the change of site from Pôrto Alegre to Evian, making impossible a direct dialog.

(28) On the basis of a study of the preparatory material, the group was able to define some general areas of common concern which must be taken into consideration both by Lutherans and by Baptists and Methodists in any future conversation. Among them are the challenge of a secular ecumenism (cf. Section II, Subsection 4, particularly para. 47), which seems to be our common task, and the historical-critical questions that are central themes for contemporary theology.

(29) In view of our common mission as Christians in the world, there are two principal questions that must be raised with urgency in the relationship between Lutherans, Methodists, and Baptists: "What is the special contribution of Lutheranism?", and "What are the special contributions of the others?"

(30) In our age denominational affiliation and confessional loyalty are being confronted by new concerns. The world now asks Lutherans, Methodists, and Baptists alike whether in their Christian discipleship they realize true humanity. The study material offered to the group revealed clearly that Baptists and Methodists are particularly concerned about this problem.

(31) The divisions among western Christians are of little interest to those in other parts of the world. The search for consensus in doctrine must be made in awareness of the other divisions which set men against each other (social, economic, political, and racial injustice) and which should be overcome for the sake of Christ. The church must accept its proper role in society with respect to the quality of life.

(32) Where Lutherans, Baptists, and Methodists are living together in their missionary situations, they have learned that proclamation of the gospel is

not restricted to verbal communication. Deeds of love can be an effective witness to the gospel.

II. *Baptists*

(33) For a long time the Lutherans have equated all Baptists with the Anabaptists of the sixteenth century, and in maintaining these one-sided judgments, have misunderstood their intentions. We must learn to see these brethren with new eyes. They can inspire us with their deep spirituality and their lively sense of community.

(34) The confrontation with the Baptists will surely raise some sharp questions about Lutheran theology and practice. For example:

a) Present development shows that more and more Lutheran churches, especially in Europe, will need to learn from the Baptist experience of functioning in the style of a "free church".

b) Baptists wonder that Lutherans baptize their children and sometimes make no serious effort to bring them up in a living relationship with the church.

c) Baptists detect what appears to be a contradiction between the Lutheran doctrine of the priesthood of believers and Lutheran practice.

III. *Methodists*

(35) Because of the evident relationships between Lutheran pietism and Methodism in its origin and because of the interest shown by many Methodist theologians in Luther's thought, dialog between Methodists and Lutherans urgently needs to be initiated.

(36) Methodists and Lutherans represent two different approaches to confessional commitment. Clarification of these differences should be one of the major concerns of this dialog. Because neither Methodism nor Lutheranism has the kind of internal homogeneity they once had, any effort to determine their relationships now will have to examine contemporary life, teaching, and mission of the churches as well as their classical documents.

(37) A Methodist theologian, José C. Miguez Bonino, whose study document we recommend for publication in *Lutheran World*, reminds us that Lutheranism and Methodism "confront each other only as institutional structures shaped by a historical process in which theological-confessional as well as other factors have been at work, particularly in the sixteenth to eighteenth centuries, giving them certain features which, in the present historical situation, become more and more indistinguishable. Certainly, one would gladly admit and confess that this historical process is not without theological significance. We believe that in and through and under this process

God raised us up as his witnesses." He also admonishes us that we must "seek together those forms of local and universal visibility which will best express . . . the missional and koinonial calling of the people of God in faithfulness to the Gospel".

Subsection 3: The Extension of Our Ecumenical Encounter—Pentecostal Churches

(38) Preparation for the discussion consisted of a lecture by Professor Nils Bloch-Hoell and a document on theological issues in Pentecostalism prepared by Dr. Walter Hollenweger. It was enriched by the contribution from Rev. Manuel de Mello, President of the Igreja Evangélica Pentecostal "O Brasil para Cristo" and the Rev. Jacques d'Avila, Vice-President of the church.

(39) The Lutheran churches have long neglected the questions posed by Pentecostal brothers in the faith. The road toward fruitful dialog has seemed to be strewn with insurmountable obstacles. Professor Nils Bloch-Hoell has claimed that "no other non-Catholic church is further removed from the Pentecostal churches than the Lutheran". One great impediment for such dialog has been the fact that Lutherans and Pentecostals know very little about each other.

(40) In recent years the ecumenical climate in the Pentecostal movement has changed decisively. Pentecostalism has come to be recognized as one of the most powerful Christian missionary forces in the world. Information about Pentecostal churches has been vastly increased through the publications of Catholic, Protestant, and nonchristian scholars. Regional consultations between Pentecostal and other church leaders have taken place in countries as different as Brazil and Rumania. In many nations Pentecostals are members of either evangelical or national councils, and three Pentecostal denominations have entered the World Council of Churches.

(41) The Pentecostal movement began not more than 70 years ago. Today it is one of the great denominational families; estimates on the number of Pentecostals in the world range from 14 to 35 million. The growth rate in Brazil, for example, has been phenomenal; beginning only in 1910, the churches today count more than 4,000,000 members. It is also significant that Pentecostalism is present in the socialist countries of Europe.

(42) Another important factor for our consideration is the development of Pentecostal manifestations in the historical churches. This movement of charismatic renewal has appeared especially in Roman Catholic, Anglican, Presbyterian, Lutheran, and Baptist circles. It has been claimed that no section of the United States, for example, is without its Roman Catholic Pentecostal prayer groups. Some academic circles have been especially receptive to the movement.

(43) We therefore believe that the time has come for the LWF to take measures to initiate a dialog between Pentecostalism and Lutheranism for the following reasons:

   a) The Spirit of God calls us to an expression of the unity which is given to us already in Christ Jesus. We recognize that Pentecostalism is a vigorous part of the church universal, nourished on basic elements of catholic faith; it is not just a marginal movement alongside the church.

   b) The Lutheran churches have been challenged from many quarters, not only from the activity of Pentecostalism, to restudy their own understanding of the Holy Spirit. Lutherans and Pentecostals each participate in their own way in the gifts of the Spirit and must share with each other their understanding of these divine gifts.

   c) Lutheranism has much to contribute from its tradition to this conversation; for example, on the doctrine of justification and the understanding of Scripture.

   d) Lutheranism should consider with Pentecostalism such matters as: the dynamics of faith; spontaneity in Christian life and worship; charismatic gifts; the nature and practice of lay ministries; different patterns of evangelism resulting in lively growth; the active participation of the people in the worship event; the appeal to the poor, humble, and the disinherited in society; and the importance of an indigenous liturgy, theology, church order, and administration; as well as financial and administrative independence from foreign church bodies.

   e) The dialog has in fact already begun on regional levels.

(44) In preparation for a truly fruitful dialog, Lutherans should give special consideration to the question of a dialogic procedure. The prospect of a dialog with Pentecostalism offers the challenge of developing a method of theological reflection which is appropriate to both partners in the dialog. This means that we must be willing to think of a dialogical method which includes common experiences in worship and life.

(45) The oral invitation from President de Mello to hold a Lutheran-Pentecostal conference in Brazil next year should be viewed favorably and explored as a step on the road to dialog.

Subsection 3: The Extension of Our Ecumenical Encounter—Independent Christian Movements

(46) The rapid growth of the so-called "independent Christian movements" in Latin America and the phenomenal proliferation of similar groups in Southern and Western Africa and elsewhere, present an unavoidable challenge to the Lutheran Church and the ecumenical family of churches

80

as a whole. Various attempts have been made to find the basic cause of the origin and development of these movements. It is now recognized that a number of causes have contributed to this complex situation. Some are as follows:

a) Sociological: racism and tribal tension, long range effects of urbanization and industrialization, the clash of cultures, and the contrast between the poor and the rich.

b) Psychological: the search for identity in stress situations; desires for their own expression of faith, for a feeling of belonging, and for the healing effects of religion; personal dissatisfaction with religious leaders; and the desire to be a leader.

c) Theological: the concern for an indigenous theology and spiritual life.

Subsection 4: Secular Ecumenism

(47) Secular ecumenism is an expression of the disillusionment of younger as well as older people over the results of ecumenical activity to the present time, and also a conscious awakening to the need for common action on urgent world problems, in which Christians of all confessions find themselves working beside nonchristians as never before. Such cooperative activity presents the danger that the church may fall into a secularist ideology, but we should not assume that this outcome is inevitable.

(48) Christians are freed by the gospel to be critical of adherence to petrified and unjust structures as well as of utopianism. Christians must also remember that sin and forgiveness of sin have decisive significance both for the social realm and for individual human existence.

(49) The false alternatives between sound doctrine and correct practice must be rejected, for doctrine and practice belong together in the deepest sense. Too often, both in the history and the present life of the church, they have been torn apart.

(50) The influence of the churches should be so applied that through the cooperation of Christians and nonchristians the structures and mechanisms of society can be changed so that the love of God may be transmitted through them.

(51) Christians today, as in the past, find themselves confronted by problems whose solutions cannot be lifted directly from the Bible or their confessions. Today, however, these problems are so urgent that Christians must learn to cooperate with all men of good will in attempting their solution. The credibility of the Christian witness is at stake if theological reflection on

the meaning of the gospel is not combined with earnest attention to social and political problems. Common reflection upon these urgent human problems may do as much to draw the divided churches together as the traditional approach toward settling doctrinal controversies has done.

RECOMMENDATIONS OF SECTION II, INCLUDING ACTIONS TAKEN BY THE ASSEMBLY

Fellowship Among Lutheran Churches and Union Negotiations (Subsection 2A)

In order to express more fully the fellowship within the LWF it is recommended:

a) that the Assembly recommend to member churches and recognized congregations that they declare through their competent authorities that they are in altar and pulpit fellowship with all member churches. Such a declaration should be made known to the General Secretary in order that it may be communicated to other member churches.

> *On the recommendation of the PRC the Assembly voted to adopt this recommendation (see item 33b of the minutes, p 142).*

Baptists and Methodists (Subsection 3A)

We recommend that the Commission on Studies be charged with the responsibility of:

a) promoting and assisting the Lutheran-Baptist and the Lutheran-Methodist dialog,

b) encouraging this dialog especially on local and regional levels where these churches are living in similar missionary situations.

> *On the recommendation of the PRC the Assembly voted to transmit the recommendation to the Executive Committee together with the opinion that present responsibilities for the Commission on Studies for dialog not be endangered (see item 33b of the minutes, p. 142).*

Pentecostal Churches (Subsection 3B)

We recommend:

a) that the Commission on Studies undertake a study of Pentecostalism,

b) that the LWF be willing to send official observers, when invited, to regional and international Pentecostal conferences, in the spirit of this declaration.

> *On the recommendation of the PRC the Assembly voted to transmit this recommendation to the new Executive Committee with the understanding that this proposal will be pursued to the extent that resources permit and, if undertaken, should cover the relationship between Lutherans and Pentecostals (see item 33b of the minutes, p. 142).*

Independent Christian Movements (Subsection 3C)

The rapid growth of the "independent Christian movements" mainly in Southern Africa and Brazil, which appear partly as Christian healing movements and sometimes show syncretistic tendencies, present a challenge to the Lutheran churches, especially by their forms of worship life. Keeping in mind the local situation including local autonomy, efforts must be made to work with groups in common political, economic, and social concerns.

We therefore submit to the LWF Assembly the following recommendations:

a) Study programs on the history, structure, and present life of these "independent Christian movements" should be initiated,

b) Local parishes and churches should be encouraged to establish contacts with these groups for mutual benefit. They should be included in constructive ecumenical dialog whenever and wherever possible,

c) When they request it, students of these groups should be considered for admission to our Lutheran colleges and seminaries.

> *On the recommendation of the PRC, the Assembly voted to transmit these recommendations to the new Executive Committee without prejudice (see item 33b of the minutes, p. 142).*

SECTION III REPORT

Responsible Participation in Today's Society

Introduction

(1) Frustrated both by the structure of the Assembly and the lack of time to thoroughly discuss the issues placed before us, Section III nevertheless attempted to approach its task responsibly.

(2) The frustration we experienced appears to be symbolic of that which exists

in today's society. The outmoded policies and procedures under which we worked may be symbolic of the rigid structures in society; the obvious gap between political philosophies, cultural traditions, young and old, laity and clergy, men and women came into focus time and time again.

(3) Yet in this situation we see our churches and our world as they exist. There are strongly diverging opinions which cannot be reconciled in such a short period of time. We have been far too interested in pointing out the faults of others without seeing our own. In some instances we attempted to reach a consensus which may have blunted the language and tone of the reports. But we remain hopeful since we did begin to learn to speak together, to understand the varying perspectives, to engage in the creative use of conflicts, and to seek common judgments. It is this process which must be continued, since Section III is only the beginning of an endless task of study and action.

(4) The following subsection reports are not completed documents or polished papers. They are presented here as they were received by the Section. No one can agree with every word in each report—but that in itself is an honest reflection of our Assembly and our times. There are inconsistencies and conflicts which ought not to be covered up.

(5) Imperfect as the reports are, they reflect where we are and point the directions in which we must move. They reflect, in this rough way, certain strong commitments. Among these are:

a) The unwillingness of the church to tolerate exploitation and oppression.

b) A desire to understand better the nature of violence.

c) The resolve to set our own houses in order.

d) The pledge to ourselves to participate in the development of a more just and humane society.

It is in this spirit that the reports are presented.

Subsection 1: Education in Crisis

(6) While discussing the world educational crisis, our group has gone through the experience of what might be regarded as one of the basic reasons for this crisis: the frustration in attempting international understanding and the intercultural exchange. The diversity between the continents and the complexity of our various backgrounds have caused many misunderstandings and even irritations among us, and we therefore want to stress from the outset the urgent need to concentrate on educational efforts toward improvement of international understanding and intercultural respect.

(7) This report cannot state consensus but rather reflects a variety of observations concerning education. These observations concentrated more on general education than on church education. Yet there was unanimity with regard to the fact that there is a worldwide crisis in education to a degree which makes it imperative that the church meet it with a special effort and through fresh and creative approaches. We felt the need for a thorough reappraisal of given educational systems as well as for pioneering innovations in education. As a background paper stated: "The church can dare to experiment with new and promising forms of education to the enrichment of the total society because of its willingness to risk failure if need be."

(8) The educational crisis is indicated by the rapidly growing gulf between the educational processes and the demands which rapid social change poses to us. Knowledge explosion on the side of the rich nations, growing illiteracy on the side of the poor nations make education part of the worldwide concern for social justice. Students resist the educational systems which they regard as irrelevant and bare of convincing values. Teachers are threatened by the rapidity with which their knowledge continuously is outmoded, with the result that their students might even know better than they. Present school systems tend to foster the stratification of society and widen the gap between educational "haves" and "have-nots", both within and between nations and continents. Inherited teaching patterns have made our schools largely places of indoctrination for a particular social system in which a certain elite gains power and perpetuates it through these schools. Both churches and governments have all too often used schools to foster their own partisan goals. The student is more an object than a subject and partner in the learning process. Teachers and educational agencies have often lost contact with social reality.

(9) It is our basic conviction that we should not ask for more education, but for a different kind of education in order to overcome this crisis. We have no definition and no blueprint for this new kind of education, but we might offer a number of clues. The first is that we do not think the churches are able to cope with the educational crisis on their own. They must join in partnership with the state and many social agencies dealing with education. In this partnership the true role of the church might be described as critical and innovative—critical toward the "image of man" that determines a given educational system, innovative toward educational approaches that foster personal development and freedom in a participatory learning process as well as social responsibility toward the community. Examples of this innovative role of the church were given from various churches and continents. We think that H.E. Tödt has pointed to basic values for any true education, values for which we would use terms such as "responsibility" and "being there for others".

(10) We see a further clue for meeting the educational crisis in the new aware-

ness of the basic relationship between education and social conditions. We believe that the church must call for equality in educational opportunity for every human being, but we realize that this is primarily a question of social and political action. There is an undeniable relationship between the classroom and the community. The educational process should be organized so that each benefits from the other.

(11) In this connection we stress the need for seeing education as being a life-long process in which school is but one means of developing the fullness of the human person. The so-called nonformal educational processes in family and community call for the special attention of the church, because here may be the most significant contacts for human development for the church in the future. We have special concern in the field of family and parents' education. Above all, we want to emphasize that no educational pattern, either in general or in church education, can be imposed from one world region to another. Educational planning and development must come out of the context of a given area.

(12) Education is not an end in itself. It serves man's development for becoming free and responsible. Therefore all educational processes need to be brought into a living relationship with the life of the community, both the believing community of the church and the community of neighbor and nation. An education which only trains for certain skills or indoctrinates certain ideologies neither deserves the name education nor appeals to the student any more.

(13) But education is not everything, it is not a remedy for all human and social ills. In our group the point was made that overstressing "education" might result in magnifying knowledge and deification of intellect. We therefore confirm the view that: a) education has to deal with the totality of man and not only with his intellect, and b) the ultimate question that lies beyond the endeavors of education is the question of love and obedience. Education cannot replace man's own personal decision. Education must rather liberate him to execute his choice in love and responsibility.

Subsection 2: Demands of Social Change

(14) This report is presented in its basic, original form. It represents a certain theological perspective which to some might seem controversial. However, the issues must be clearly stated so that fruitful dialog can ensue.

(15) After an initial collection of questions the group agreed on three main aspects for the discussion: a) the nature of the structures of today's society; b) the criteria for evaluating these structures; c) the role of the church as an instrument of social change.

(16) The term "structure" did not go unchallenged, however. Some felt that it was too static and that we should regain the dynamic approach of the Bible and speak instead of functions and goals.

(17) In this connection two different points of departure were suggested:

a) One starting from the recognition that man lives in certain structures, and from there proceeding to the evaluation of these structures—their limits and their dehumanizing effects.

b) The other starting from the demands of the present situation of the world, and from there proceeding to understand the task of the church over against such demands.

In the following discussion both methods were employed in a complementary fashion. The underlying concern was very much the same; the task of the church to serve men in their concrete, present needs.

(18) Another tension which prevailed throughout the discussion was a disagreement on methodology, whether we should evolve socio-ethical principles in broad statements and leave the implementation to the individual churches in their concrete situation, or whether we should address ourselves to specific oppressive forces in certain areas of the present world situation and urge the churches and/or the LWF to take concrete action in order to enforce a change. Eventually it developed that the group agreed on accepting basic theses, leaving application to local implementation in view of the varied backgrounds of different member churches.

(19) We had no fundamental disagreement on the goals. Over against traditional Lutheranism, which had as its ethical object only the individual, we recognize that change takes place not only in and through the individual, but also, and often mainly, socially. The necessity of a corporate involvement of the church in socio-political problems was repeatedly affirmed by our group.

(20) It became obvious through the discussion of concrete instances, that the priorities for the church's social action in the world center in the areas of political power, of economic and societal power structures, and of patterns of racism.

(21) In our discussion about the structures of the present society, the following points were brought forward:

a) We recognize that men live in certain structures (patterns of relationship, social processes, or forces which shape human life). There is no unstructured vitality; life is patterned in relationship.

b) However, we deny that any particular institutional forms as they appear in history are divinely ordained. All social structures have to be understood as tools or instruments, through which man fulfills God's mandate to live in love and justice in his relationships with fellowmen. Structures are not to be seen as ends in themselves.

c) Inherent in all structures is the necessity of organizing and distributing power, which sinful man tends to abuse for self-preservation and oppression of others.

d) Therefore, it is imperative to examine all structures constantly and critically according to evaluative criteria which are in keeping with God's intention for human life.

(22) The following criteria were mentioned:

a) The essential purpose of all inevitable social structures is to serve man and enable him to live a human life.

b) Structures are misused when they make man an object of power or when they deny the basic human needs to him or to certain groups within society.

c) The term "basic human needs" was amplified to include fundamental physical needs (e.g., adequate food, housing, work), the need for freedom and justice, the need for love and esteem, the need for fellowship, and the need for self-actualization (i.e., self-expression, participation in power, etc.).

(23) In the fulfillment of its social responsibilities under God the church has three basic tasks:

a) A pastoral function in strengthening those who suffer, offering them fellowship (in co-suffering), and enabling them through the proclamation of the gospel to face their situation fearlessly.

b) An educational function in equipping and supporting the people, who through their secular role in society have the power to work toward justice and constructive social change.

c) A social and political function beyond its traditional roles, in working toward and demanding humane and just structures for society.

(24) Such responsibilities include:

a) Necessary provision of accurate, and unprejudiced, and factual information as a prerogative for decision-making and awakening of conscience.

b) Participation in the decision-making process in order to effect progress toward humane justice for all.

c) Advocating a just distribution of political power for all men in society.

d) Critical evaluation of global economic structures and distribution of resources which assist human life.

(25) The following theses are presented as a summation of our discussion and as a stimulus for further study and appropriate action within the LWF and its member churches:

(26) We affirm the existence of social structures which are meant to serve as part of God's creative intention for humane life as expressions of his love.

(27) The fundamental purpose of these social processes is to ensure the just distribution and exercise of power in all areas of life, including the political, societal, economic, and communal.

(28) We assert that no particular form of social structure is sacrosanct. Men are accountable to God for the proper use of all social structures and therefore bear responsibility for effecting constructive changes to meet emerging human needs.

(29) Criteria for change are derived from an evaluation of the degree to which any given social structure ensures peace, justice, freedom, and other basic human rights.

(30) In obedience to the living Lord of history, specific social structures are to be supported when they provide the just means for man to serve his neighbor. They should be denied such support and changed or replaced, either when they cannot be used in service to one's neighbor or when they exist merely for self-preservation or self-aggrandizement.

(31) The calling of the church into the world requires that it be actively involved in constructive social change. In doing so, the church itself stands under both the judgment and grace of God.

(32) In its involvement in social change, the church should adopt both a judgmental and reconciling stance toward all those involved in the social structures being challenged.

(33) The church has often been viewed in terms of permanence and stability in the midst of transience. This misunderstanding by both church and world has been interpreted to mean that the church is the uncritical upholder of the *status quo*. However, the church's obedience to God's ongoing activity in history requires that she act as an advocate of positive social change.

(34) The church, which is not fearful of involvement in effective social change, expresses itself in a variety of ways:

a) The church may act both corporately and through its individual members. Both of these approaches are valid and ought to be utilized as the specific situation may allow. However, the increasing corporate complexity of modern society requires increased corporate action on the part of the church.

b) The church, trusting in God's promise of renewal, should call both the world and itself to accountability and service through its worship, teaching, proclamation, and diaconic ministry.

c) The church witnesses to its commitment in social change by its willingness to arrange its own structures so that they are not only sensitive to human need, but also demonstrate the responsible use of power in the service of others.

d) The church may become involved in strategies of radical transformation directed toward institutions and structures which oppress and dehumanize powerless individuals and groups. No single method of change can be identified with the fulfillment of Christian social responsibility. It is judgment based on the heritage of the Christian faith, the facts of the situation, the methods necessary and the hoped-for goals, which will determine the course of action to be taken. In the fulfillment of its social task, the church eagerly joins hands with all men of good will to promote justice and to relieve human misery. Christians are grateful for all just structures of government in which they can exercise their social responsibility.

(35) The church, as it seeks to fulfill its social responsibility, should avail itself of pertinent factual information and promote open channels of communication between all sectors of society.

Subsection 3: Economic Justice and Human Rights

(36) Discussion centered primarily on the reality of economic injustice, its causes and its unfortunate effect on elementary human rights. Even more significantly, it dealt with ways and means of overcoming economic injustice as well as the role of the churches in assisting the process.

(37) Particular effort was made to reconcile possible rhetorical differences in order to arrive, if possible, at agreement regarding the substance of our Christian concern for our fellowmen in need or distress.

(38) The following report embraces two main parts: first, an account of the dis-

cussion on economic justice and, second, the results of the debate on human rights.

I. *Economic Justice*

(39) The implications of the subject "economic justice" were given considerable attention throughout all the sessions.

Three basic points were made:

(40) First: Relief work in its narrow sense should by no means be abandoned, although it was asked whether it sometimes does not receive too much emphasis in the whole field of economic justice in which the churches are working. It was also understood that such aid is supplementary in emergency situations—not a substitute for measures to increase development or for an attack on the root-causes of economic injustice.

(41) Second: It was recognized that a clearer understanding about the root-causes of underdevelopment, hunger, misery, etc., is necessary. No clear consensus emerged as to the character of such causes and the methods for overcoming them. Two basic approaches, however, were distinguishable. One asked for concrete steps in concrete situations and stressed that overall economic consideration should be left to experts in the field. Whenever human needs are evident the church and the Christian should act. The other approach stressed the necessity of a much wider general understanding of the mechanisms and structures that, first of all, at an international level created or maintained economic injustice. It was held that the present situation of underdevelopment can be traced back to colonialist origins and that they still constitute a vicious circle whereby present patterns of economic wealth of a world minority increase the misery of a majority of the world population. This approach also pointed out that the introduction of processes which were once used by the industrialized countries is not only useless but harmful. They can only contribute to a growing domination, a widening gap between the "rich" and the "poor", an unjust international division of labor, and a distorted and externally controlled economy in the countries of the Third World.

(42) Third: Economic factors, however, were not seen as the only dominant ones. Great stress was also laid on education. But here again the consensus was not clear. Some stressed that education (instruction) *per se* creates the basic conditions for the humanizing process. Others felt that education could never be taken as something which is purely factual or neutral, but is always something which is political. It was pointed out by some that traditional education is geared toward adjusting man to the *status quo* and that for this reason it is necessary to foster man's ability to create and transform. It is necessary to awaken man's awareness of his own

situation, its causes, and new possibilities. At any rate, education promoted by the churches should aim at a change of mentality, which would include in it a greater critical awareness of the human problems involved in living in this world. This work must begin with considerable insight into the immediate social context and must be promoted by communication of information at all levels.

II. *Human Rights*

(43) The discussion of human rights occurred in the light of problems of economic injustice, because we realized that violence against humanity in today's societies, generally speaking, has its source in economic structures. This fact determines the way in which the problems of human rights must be seen today; the approach can no longer be exclusively that of protecting the individual. The social and political obligation to create relationships based on human values has moved into the foreground. Formally declared human rights (U.N. Declaration, etc.) implicitly contain the obligation for states and societies to create and maintain—through constructive development of their internal order—the conditions under which human rights can be realized in an explicit sense. This requires a dynamic review, as well as a continuing development of human rights. That does not change the basic and normative principle of human rights. If the integrity and dignity of the individual constitute the kernel of human rights, the same remains the criterion for the extension and amendment of human rights under changing social and economic conditions.

(44) Therefore, we are definitely of the opinion that the churches and the LWF should support the significance of human rights with all their influence. They should appropriate them in a Christian sense and work toward their fulfillment.

(45) This task places Christians and the churches in the position to cooperate in all areas with nonchristians regardless of ideology. Moreover, the churches should cooperate in the development of an international ethos and a body of international law, which will give form to the protective and constructive function of law for the coexistence of states in service to mankind.

(46) Particular violations of human rights, above all the torture of political prisoners, should arouse immediate protest from the churches regardless of the political regime or the loyalty of churches with respect to it. In view of the examples of violations of human rights, such as those with which the LWF was confronted in connection with the proposed Assembly location in Brazil, the following question calls for study: what basis in church tradition or elsewhere caused us to react hesitantly and ambiguously to these matters? The churches should not now push this problem aside, but rather examine critically whether in their own actions they really take seriously the obligations of human rights.

(47) The same applies also to other human freedoms, such as conscientious objection to military service or questions of racial discrimination.

(48) The problem of race relations, or how to improve intergroup relations, is a major and urgent issue with which the church must deal out of Christian concern. Historically, those in our society who look different, who are weak and lacking power, have been treated differently. As a first step, the church should face the fact that it has often been exclusive toward groups of people and that the energies of the church should now be extended as fully as possible toward overcoming past injustices.

(49) We are confronted by an intensification of racism—both in its institutional and personal forms—in almost every part of the world. This matter is much deeper than race, for it also includes the profound discrimination between people of the same race who have different cultures. Whether it be the horrendous system of apartheid and colonialism as it exists in Southern Africa, or the continuing racial tension in the United States, or the discrimination against migrant laborers in Switzerland, or the extreme poverty of Indians in Canada—the fact remains that racism is an insidious method which denies human rights to many.

(50) We recognize that many of our Christian brethren in these places are making significant efforts to change these systems, and it is these efforts that we support and to which we hope the LWF will make a substantial contribution as soon as possible.

(51) Although it is urgent that race relations be improved throughout the world, the race situation within the continental United States needs the church's immediate attention.

(52) The issues in need of urgent attention are: the improvement of police-community relations; ways and means of providing adequate housing on a nonsegregated basis; the willingness of the church to assess the existing educational system, and to assist in providing better and improved educational opportunities for all people.

(53) Furthermore, improvement of the system of medical care is of concern, for this must be organized and clarified so that all persons will be able to take full advantage of health services.

(54) An adequate standard of living as a right of the individual should be preserved; the Christian community should help maintain a level below which no human being should have to live. The welfare system must be undergirded by the church so that the material needs of the less fortunate can be met.

(55) Employment and the right of the individual to secure employment op-

portunities in keeping with his ability (without race being a factor) is a goal to which the church should commit itself.

Conclusion

(56) Having thus affirmed the close interrelationship between economic justice and human rights, we urgently commend these considerations to the LWF and its member churches throughout the world, not only for study but for concrete action.

Subsection 4: Servanthood and Peace

(57) The expansion of crises such as those in Vietnam and the Middle East, as well as the increasing tensions between dominating and dominated classes and races, threatens to transform the state of latent conflict into a phase of open international conflict.

(58) Violence, overt and hidden, in its many forms, armed aggression for legitimate and illegitimate change, oppression to maintain perverted political-social structures—all are permanent threats to elementary security and peace.

(59) Into this world the churches are being sent to serve the cause of peace. The peace which the Christians seek must be seen in its two dimensions: reconciliation between man and God, and reconciliation between man and man.

(60) Peace cannot mean simply absence of war, nor can it be the maintenance of the *status quo* either by power structures or by military armament; rather, it is a style of life which embodies creative humanization. It is a dynamic process by which we must be challenged. It requires the responsible participation of everybody involved in a given situation.

(61) Therefore, the maintenance of peace requires a stategy for peace oriented toward the future. This must take into account its many dimensions, such as social and economic justice, human rights, as well as reconciliation, mutual respect, and mutual recognition.

(62) We need to reconsider a number of traditional attitudes in order to understand that Christians, both individually and corporately, must be engaged in political processes which include, but also go beyond, national structures.

(63) In view of Romans 13 we must ask, what is "legitimate authority"? Is it the government of a country, a regional organization, the UNO? In the context of our understanding of civil authority and the need for this authority, we as Lutherans have a unique contribution to make.

(64) The churches should be willing to become involved in the struggle of political systems, whenever these are perverted. They should be conscious of their responsibility to stand up against any perversion on all sides and all fronts.

(65) This may mean encouraging our people to offer themselves, both for civil service work in government, national, regional or international organizations, and as volunteers in special organizations serving peace.

(66) This may also mean spurring churches on to develop models of peace structures—in cooperation with other men of good will who are also concerned for peace, justice, and human rights.

(67) We take note of the activity of certain churches in recognizing and supporting the right of general and selective conscientious objection to war.

(68) This requires a reevaluation of our educational programs with the question in mind as to what extent they serve peace (cf. The Ecumenical Peace Council of Holland).

(69) In case of war or conflict the churches' charitable services should be extended to all in need without regard to the parties involved (as is done by the Department of World Service of the LWF).

(70) Addressing the world and primarily our own governments, we must urge them to reconsider their national priorities: armament or human development? In addition we must urge them to give up a certain amount of national sovereignty in the interest of world community.

(71) Thus, the UNO should be strengthened and enlarged on the basis of the principle of its universality and of the maximum responsible participation of all. The two Chinas, the two Koreas, the two Germanies, etc. should be admitted as members, and the Declaration of Human Rights should definitely be made more effective.

(72) There are presently several painful and explosive situations confronting the world. Among these are the continuation of the Vietnam War, the continuation of conflict in the Middle East, and the strengthening of military regimes as seen in Greece and South America. The continuation of these conditions can only lead to an exceedingly dangerous situation for all mankind. As Christians we must both raise our voices in strong protest and engage in efforts to find just solutions to these dangerous problems. We commend the position taken by the churches in the United States vis-à-vis their government as they work toward a cessation of the war in Vietnam. Within the context of world peace every effort should be supported which seeks to set up security on regional levels, such as that undertaken in Europe.

(73) War, as an instrument of national policy for settling a dispute, can no longer be tolerated without protest.

RECOMMENDATIONS OF SECTION III, INCLUDING ACTIONS TAKEN BY THE ASSEMBLY

Crisis in Education (Knowledge Explosion and Technological Revolution) (Subsection 1)

We support the recommendations of the Commission on Education to the new Executive Committee*

The suggested amendments to the recommendations of the Commission on Education to the new Executive Committee, on recommendation of the PRC, were transmitted by Assembly action to the new Executive Committee without prejudice (see item 33a of the minutes, p. 141).

Demands of Social Change (Subsection 2)

Resolution regarding conferences on Social Responsibility

WHEREAS, World Lutheran Conferences on Social Responsibility (Springfield, Ohio, 1956; Stockholm, Sweden, 1963; and Regional Conferences in Addis Ababa, Africa; Caracas, Venezuela, and Baden, Austria, 1969) have proved helpful both in furthering understanding of the diaconic task of the church, and in preparation for LWF assemblies, and;

WHEREAS, the dimensions and complexity of the diaconic task are rapidly increasing, requiring ongoing discussions and planning between representatives of Lutheran churches throughout the world;

Therefore, be it resolved that:

1. Section III recommend to the Assembly that an appropriate office of the LWF be authorized to call into session both world and regional conferences in social responsibility during the next two years.

2. LWF ask its Department of World Service to consider ways and means to provide consultation for churches which desire assistance in developing social action programs.

On the recommendation of the PRC, the Assembly voted to transmit these recommendations to the new Executive Committee without prejudice (see item 33b of the minutes, p. 142).

---

* These recommendations appear as Appendix 5 of the Executive Committee Report and Recommendations (Document 18) which is available upon request from the *General Secretary, Lutheran World Federation, 150 route de Ferney, 1211 Geneva 20, Switzerland.*

Economic Justice and Human Rights (Subsection 3)

1. Racial Issues and Minority Problems

> *This statement in revised form was adopted by the Assembly (cf. item 64 of the minutes, p. 161).*

2. Causes of Underdevelopment, World Hunger, and Misery

Section III noted the progress in the scope of World Service in Community Development, following not only traditional patterns, but also applying new project concepts and partnerships. This growing involvement of World Service in development, calls for a continuing awareness of social-political factors relevant to such activities. Accordingly, the Section accepted the following statement:

Causes of Underdevelopment, World Hunger, and Misery

We must be aware that growing circles—experts and otherwise—are interpreting available data as follows:

1. The problem of underdevelopment, misery, and poverty is not an isolated event from colonial history which, it is held, is still in operation through a number of economic, political, social, and cultural mechanisms.

2. Therefore, it is held in consequence, that the "catching up" theory—namely the accelerated imitation of the methods used by today's so-called developed countries is not feasible. On the contrary, such an attempt would only contribute to a growing domination, a widening gap between the "rich and the poor", an unjust international division of labor and a distorted and externally controlled economy in most countries of the Third World.

3. Therefore, also, if the foregoing analysis is correct, deep-going changes must be brought about on two levels, both

a) in the rich countries (especially with respect to their present international trade practices) etc., and

b) in the underdeveloped countries. Here, socio-political changes are needed to bring about a wide participation by their peoples in the decision-making processes. Also the ruling minorities that allegedly benefit from the present system in detriment to the genuine national interests of their countries have to be neutralized and replaced.

We understand that such an analysis—because of its acceptance by many experts and political forces in the Third World and even outside it—cannot

97

simply be dismissed. That would not lead to any meaningful reconciliation but would only sharpen the polarization and, in the last instance, perhaps even endanger world peace.

We must also be aware that a rejection of such a position would not be equivalent to an "objective" or "neutral" stand but simply signifies taking a different political (ideological) position.

(The text to this point was to have been submitted by the PRC to the Resolutions Committee, but neither this text nor a substitute was subsequently submitted to the plenary.)

In the light of all that we recommend:

a) That the structure of World Service be strengthened and changed in such a manner that partnership between donors and receivers be guaranteed. It is important that representation on agencies of the LWF and on its staff be more representative of all the member churches—particularly those of the Third World. Selection of such personnel should not be related principally to the size of contributions of certain member churches, which now appears to be the case. It remains a constant challenge to the older established churches to give priority to the needs and wishes of the younger developing churches and to lay aside their own church-political interests.

On the recommendation of the PRC, and after amendment, the Assembly adopted the following substitute recommendation:

In order to ensure that the international and fraternal character of the LWF is increasingly reflected in its staffing policy, by representation on LWF organs and in the relationship between member churches and in the agencies, it is recommended:

1. That every endeavor be made to make representation on LWF organs and staff more representative of all member churches, particularly those of Africa, Asia, and Latin America.

2. That the older, well established and financially strong LWF member churches be challenged to remain constantly aware of the needs and aspirations of the churches in the developing countries.

3. That the LWF member churches in Asia, Africa, and Latin America be encouraged to release qualified personnel for service with the LWF in order that an adequate number of staff members from these regions will be available for staff appointments.

4. That through its Scholarship Program and other means, the LWF assist churches in Asia, Africa, and Latin America in the training of

qualified personnel both for their internal requirements and for appointment to LWF and other ecumenical organizations.

b) That the work of the World Service Department be provided, through proper mechanism, with guidelines and criteria embracing:

1. Basic ideological considerations and models in the field of social and economic development.

2. Study of the involvement of the church in society. What it is? What should it be? What changes can be brought about?

3. Carry out (where possible) case studies on more projects of the World Service program. How does it relate to national and international development in a political and ideological sense?

Such analyses should also relate critically to established churches, World Service programs and government projects.

It is also our concern that there be dialog between youth and adults both in the preparation and in the field.

On the recommendation of the PRC, the Assembly voted to transmit this recommendation to the new Executive Committee for consideration.

c) It is further recommended that, in cooperation with the Study Department, a strategy of assistance be developed with the goal that the right of self-determination of the underprivileged may become politically effective in the framework of a universal order of peace.

On the recommendation of the PRC, the Assembly voted to transmit this recommendation to the new Executive Committee for consideration.

3. Human Rights Declaration

A revised statement (cf. item 38b of the minutes p. 145) was adopted by the Assembly (cf. item 44 of the minutes, p. 147).

Servanthood and Peace (Subsection 4)

Introduction

The present world situation comprises a profusion of conflicts which threaten civilizations and require active steps toward peace. In our opinion, peace denotes a continual challenge to the shaping of the dynamic processes of society in the best possible way. For this reason, a *multidimensional, dynamic strategy for peace* is necessary. Participation in this strategy grows out of the task of achieving peace and reconciliation on the part of Christians who have been reconciled by God. This strategy touches three levels above all:

1. Critical and dynamic effort on behalf of social structures which guarantee the greatest justice. Conflicts which lead to war are rooted, among other places, in the injustice inhering in relationships. A peace maintained only by force is a negative peace which begets even greater conflicts and the absence of peace.

2. Further, strategy toward peace involves dismantling particular national, bloc-related military systems in east and west and building worldwide systems of security and law.

3. This strategy touches a level of nonviolent action.

I. *The Section proposal in slightly revised form was adopted by the Assembly as a Statement on Servanthood and Peace (cf. item 63 of the minutes, p. 160).*

II. We recommend that the LWF establish a project within its structure that would enable a cooperation with the effort undertaken by other organizations to investigate and communicate strategies toward dynamic peace.

That the project include these aspects:

1. A ministry to those who object to military service to be coordinated and initiated by the LWF. This should include:

   a. A working committee to establish guidelines and define staff portfolios.

   b. Communication about participation and involvement in existing projects by member churches and other organizations.

   c. Direct contact with persons involved in all phases of these concerns.

   d. Development of alternative service opportunities

      a) within the United Nations (peace and development frame work) and local, national or international church projects.

      b) in peace educational projects.

      c) Lutheran World Federation Refugee Services be extended to those who emigrate because of objection in principle to either all military services or to a specific war.

2. That this ministry be related to all education activities of the LWF.

   Upon the recommendation of the PRC, the Assembly voted to transmit this recommendation to the new Executive Committee (cf. item 33b of the minutes, p. 142).

Abridged Minutes of the Plenary Sessions of the Fifth Assembly of the Lutheran World Federation

(including Resolutions, Recommendations and Statements)[1]

Plenary I
Tuesday morning
July 14, 1970

(1) Opening of the Assembly

> Dr. Fredrik A. Schiotz (USA), President of the Lutheran World Federation declared the Fifth Assembly of the LWF open and welcomed all participants.

> Archbishop Martti Simojoki (Finland) chaired the session during the President's Opening Address.

(2) Opening Address: Dr. Fredrik A. Schiotz (see pp. 20-30)

> President Schiotz prefaced his Opening Address with an introductory statement. During the reading of paragraphs 4 and 5 of the introductory statement some delegates rose and put on black armbands, apparently as a sign of protest to certain statements concerning Brazil. The Opening Address was greeted by applause. The chairman, Archbishop Simojoki, announced that the text of the Opening Address would be referred to the Policy and Reference Committee.

(3) The Associate General Secretary gave a short orientation on the Assembly structure, program, and materials.

> In response to a question from the floor, the President gave the assurance that when the agenda is adopted amendments to the agenda could be submitted to the Business Committee which would report both the request for amendment and its proposal to the Assembly.

(4) Presentation by the Executive Committee

> a) The agenda as submitted was adopted.

Plenary II
Tuesday afternoon
July 14, 1970

> b) The Rules of Procedure as proposed by the Executive Committee were

---

[1] The Unabridged Minutes are available upon request from the General Secretary, LWF, 150 route de Ferney, 1211 Geneva 20, Switzerland. All Statements and Resolutions officially adopted by the Assembly are printed in bold face type.

presented. Certain amendments were proposed. The Rules of Procedure as amended were adopted. The President called attention to the fact that rulings by the chair may be challenged by simple majority vote.

c) The Report of the Executive Committee and

d) The Reports of the Commissions and Committees of the LWF for the period 1963-1969 were referred to the Policy and Reference Committee (PRC).

e) Applications for Membership

Bishop Birkeli (Norway), chairman of the Membership Committee of the Executive Committee, presented the report. By unanimous vote the following churches were received into membership in the LWF:

(1) India Evangelical Lutheran Church

(2) Huria Kristen Indonesia (Indonesian Christian Church)

(3) Evangelical Lutheran Church in South-West Africa (Rhenish Mission Church)

(4) Lutheran Church of Kenya

The delegates of these churches who were present were received with applause. The delegation of the Huria Kristen Indonesia expressed its gratitude to the Executive Committee and to the Assembly for this action. The President was honored by this delegation with a Batak shawl.

f) Appointment of Assembly Committees

The President asked the General Secretary to present the nominations of the Executive Committee for standing, section steering, and ad hoc committees, commenting that the nominations took into account adequate geographical representation. He reported that criticism has been expressed at the World Encounter of Lutheran Youth concerning the nomination process. Criticisms were then raised from the floor, the president suggesting that a concrete proposal for changing this process could be formulated and submitted to the PRC for its consideration.

The nominations of members to the following committees, as amended by common consent, were put to the vote and the following persons elected:

A. Policy and Reference Committee
(chairman, 4 Executive Committee members and 12 delegates)

1. Mikko JUVA	Finland	Chairman
2. Fridtjov BIRKELI	Norway	
3. Ingo BRAECKLEIN	GDR	
4. Manas BUTHELEZI	South Africa	
5. Bo GIERTZ	Sweden	
6. Sophia HUANG	Taiwan	
7. Zoltan KALDY	Hungary	
8. Judah B. M. KIWOVELE	Tanzania	
9. Jørgen LISSNER	Denmark	
10. Robert J. MARSHALL	USA	
11. C. Bimal MINZ	India	
12. Luvern V. RIEKE	USA	
13. Gustavo RODRIGUEZ	Colombia	
14. Kurt SCHMIDT-CLAUSEN	FRG	
15. Doris L. SPONG	USA	
16. Gudina TUMSA	Ethiopia	
17. Rudolf WEEBER	FRG	

B. Nominations Committee
(chairman, 16 delegates)

1. Andrzej WANTULA	Poland	Chairman
2. Rakoto ANDRIANARIJAONA	Madagascar	
3. Juan COBRDA	Argentina	
4. Gustav DIEHL	India	
5. Ulrich FICK	FRG	
6 Reinhard GLEISNER	Chile	
7. George HARKINS	USA	
8. Fritz HEIDLER	GDR	
9. Wolfgang HELBIG	FRG	
10. Marc LIENHARD	France	
11. Joel NGEIYAMU	Tanzania	
12. Daniel RAPOO	South Africa	
13. Herman SCHLYTER	Sweden	
14. George SCHULTZ	USA	
15. Bodil SØLLING	Denmark	
16. Sueaki UTSUMI	Japan	
17. Rebecca S. VOIGTS	Canada	

C. Resolutions Committee
(chairman, 6 delegates)

1. Paul EMPIE   USA   Chairman
2. Kurapati D. BENJAMIN India
3. Antti HAUTAMÄKI   Finland
4. Janis MATULIS   Latvia (USSR)
5. Adolf SPERL   FRG
6. Per VOKSØ   Norway
7. Cuthbert OMARI   Tanzania

D. Credentials and Elections Committee
(chairman, 8 delegates)

1. Roland PAYNE   Liberia   Chairman
2. Donald Frank
   GRUENBURG   USA
3. C. F. G. Eddy
   HALLEWAS   Netherlands
4. Edgar HARK   Estonia (USSR)
5. Lois JOSEFSON   USA
6. Apaisaria LYIMO   Tanzania
7. Traugott OHSE   GDR
8. Detlef RÖTTING   FRG
9. Birger SWENSON   Sweden

E. Minutes Committee
(chairman, 4 delegates)

1. Earl TREUSCH   Canada   Chairman
2. Wolfgang ENGE   Italy
3. Felix MODEROW   GDR
4. Dorairaj PETER   India
5. Keflejesus TESEMMA   Ethiopia (not in
                                  attendance)

F. Business Committee
The Business Committee consists of the Executive Committee members and section chairmen:

1. Emmanuel ABRAHAM   Ethiopia   Section III
2. Enok ÅDNØY   Norway   Section I
3. Leonard AUALA   South-West Africa Executive Committee
4. Fridtjov BIRKELI   Norway   "   "
5. Hermann
   DIETZFELBINGER   FRG (not in
                          attendance)   "   "

6. Bo GIERTZ	Sweden	"	"
7. Karl GOTTSCHALD	Brazil (not in attendance)	"	"
8. Etienne JUNG	France	"	"
9. Friedrich-Wilhelm KRUMMACHER	GDR	" "	" "
10. Jens LEER-ANDERSEN	Denmark	"	"
11. Hanns LILJE	FRG	"	"
12. Robert J. MARSHALL	USA	"	"
13. Norman A. MENTER	USA	"	"
14. Stefano R. MOSHI	Tanzania	"	"
15. Warren A. QUANBECK	USA	Section II	
16. Wolfgang SCHANZE	GDR	Executive Committee	
17. Fredrik A. SCHIOTZ	USA	"	"
18. Gerhard SILITONGA	Indonesia	"	"
19. Martti SIMOJOKI	Finland	"	"
20. Clarence W. SORENSEN	USA (not in attendance)	"	"
21. Andrzej WANTULA	Poland	"	"
22. Rudolf WEEBER	FRG	"	"

(5) First Report of the Credentials Committee (for Final Report see item 51)

(6) Greetings from the Churches of France

The following persons representing churches of the country in which the Assembly was meeting brought greetings:

a) Pastor René Blanc, President of the Executive Committee of the Evangelical Lutheran Church of France, representing the Lutheran Churches of France,

b) President Etienne Jung, a member of the LWF Executive Committee, Vice-President of the French Protestant Federation,

c) Monseigneur Sauvage, the Bishop of Annecy, representing also the Catholic Bishops' Conference of France.

(7) Discussion on the Change of Assembly Site

a) The General Secretary read his report "From Pôrto Alegre to Evian".

It is becoming more and more difficult to arrive at unanimity within the church. Differences of opinion are rife even while we are speaking of unity; the consensus of opinion which we are striving for is giving way to "confrontations"; majority votes arouse motions of censure from the minorities. Why should the LWF be the exception to what seems to be the general rule? There is, however, at the outset of this Fifth Assembly, a unanimity which no one desired and which, owing to its negative character, could lead to dangerous results. For one reason or another we are all dissatisfied at being here and should have preferred matters to have gone differently. This is obviously not the only point which unites us, and it is essential that the discussion on the "reason why we are not assembled" in Pôrto Alegre should reveal a profound bond which neither our differences of opinion nor different ways of interpreting the facts should be able to call to account.

We owe you some explanations for what has happened during these past few months and we shall give them to you as objectively as possible—by way of an exchange, which should not show that some of us were right, and others wrong, but rather, that we all have something to learn from it. In fact, it concerns a great deal more than what some call the *storia del fracasso* and others the "victory of reason". For the first time in the history of our Federation, the preparatory period prior to an Assembly has reached far beyond the stages of an academic, theological, or even passionate discussion; it has shaken several of our churches to their very foundations; it has brought us face to face with difficult matters directly connected with the theme which we have chosen. The Assembly is not starting today, it does not only concern you, it is not only of interest to leaders of churches, but also to congregations, groups and individuals for whom the LWF was only a distant reality. We are not debating behind closed doors; the road from Pôrto Alegre to Evian is firmly situated in this complex and difficult world, strewn with hidden pitfalls, in which we live. Throughout the entire length of this road, God has endeavored to make us reflect on the meaning, for Christians, of the phrase "Sent into the World". Evian is just one stage of the journey, a stopping-place to take our bearings, an opportunity to correct our direction, and to see if we are heading toward the goal we set ourselves.

The question of whether this kind of world assembly, such as we have organized for the fifth time, is really the most effective way of going about this type of examination, is more open than ever. It is one of a great many other questions which we can no longer postpone to be studied at some future and hypothetical date. Our desire to inform the churches and public opinion of our intentions, the use of the mass media and the wishes of many of us to make known *urbi et orbi* what you are thinking and what you believe ought to be said, all this is very praiseworthy. However, I am certain that, in many respects, we are neither prepared, nor have we the necessary equipment, for a confrontation in an arena, exposed to the gusts of wind of an emotive public, and the implacable glare of the spotlights of the critics. During these past few months we were continually worried by the question of the kind of witness we ought to give in respect of the particular situation in Brazil. We cannot reply without asking ourselves if the weapons we are using for the fight really match those which the Apostle Paul lists at the end of the Epistle to the Ephesians, or whether we are trying to fight according to rules which are not really our own. Let us apply the standards which are in keeping with the gospel and which will afford us the liberty to draw the conclusions from this experience which shall not divide us, but which may even bring a little light to those who "hunger and thirst for righteousness".

It is worth reminding you of the reasons why the LWF accepted the invitation of the church in Brazil. The Executive Committee saw in it new possibilities, combined with the fact that it concerned a minority church, and that the Assembly would be held in Latin America. As a consequence of historical circumstances, Lutheranism is particularly strong in Northern Europe and the United States. In other places, where our churches have grown up as a result of emigration or the work of missionaries, they are generally smaller in size. A distinguishing mark of the LWF is the dynamism of its larger member churches and the useful relationships which these have set up with the smaller churches. We should not underestimate the echo which resounded throughout the Third World following our decision to go to Pôrto Alegre. It was an acknowledgment of the role of the minority churches within the fold of our spiritual family, it was a hope that they would make a still more positive contribution to its way of life. By our decision not to go to Pôrto Alegre, many of these churches think that everything has again been called into question. Having come to identify themselves with the host church, they now feel equally derided and crushed by the weight of those churches, which are more powerful, more noisy, and financially in a stronger position than themselves!

It is obvious that a community of churches, which is so diverse, poses many problems. Surely the role of the LWF is precisely that of watching to see that there is a constant exchange between the historic and up-to-date expressions of Lutheranism in the world. This is what we still believe and it was one of the reasons which induced the Officers of the Federation to maintain their decision to go to Pôrto Alegro for as long as possible. The experience of these last few months proves, nevertheless, that it is extremely difficult for us to disregard our own cultural and national conditioning, in order to understand and accept a new situation. We need only read the many articles written about the church in Brazil. The analyses are often correct, although sometimes exaggerated. Each one assesses it according to his own preconceived ideas, and does not always pay sufficient attention to the points of view of those directly concerned. The hollow dialog to which this has led us arises from the fact that several of those invited to take part in the Assembly wished to apply surgical methods to the situation, which were not in accordance with the wishes of the host church.

We should also bear in mind another element which goes to make up each Assembly and which is particularly desired in the case of a minority church. A world assembly is a public event, which should also reveal the existence and testimony of our communion to the masses. Pôrto Alegre should have been, for the Lutherans in Brazil, a unique occasion for showing that they belong to a larger and wider reality. The presence in their country of their brothers from all other continents, should not only have enriched them both spiritually and humanly, but should have shown, we must also admit, that Lutheranism has world-wide and universal dimensions. This gave rise to a misunderstanding which continued to grow between the LWF and the Brazilian Committee preparing for the Assembly, as the former, conscious of the evolution of the role of the church in society, and of the difficulties involved in organizing world conferences, stressed the "working" character of the Assembly, the latter were more concerned with the impact of this meeting on the public. We were trying to establish a certain tone of simplicity and restraint, quite free from any spirit of triumphalism, rendered all the more necessary in view of the fact that the political situation in Brazil increasingly called for the greatest discretion vis-à-vis the authorities. In the case of our brothers, the criticisms which were expressed in many of our churches did not reach them, or were rejected. On the other hand, the public rally in Novo Hamburgo (due to take place on July 19) was conceived as a "Kirchentag" of the 1950s and did not take into account the questions to which it has given rise in Germany during the past ten years. As for relationships between the church and the world, these were seen as being essentially channeled through the representatives of official and political institutions. More attention was given to paying one's respects to the authorities of this world, than to expressing one's solidarity with the weak, the dispossessed, and the suffering.

To be quite fair and honest, it should be stated that the organizers in Geneva should have brought more pressure to bear on the Committee preparing for the Assembly in Pôrto Alegre, to make them understand the risks they were running. We had divided the work between us and had left them complete liberty to organize the way in which they thought fit to receive their guests individually and the Assembly in general. It is impossible to imagine the impact on the public of a world conference as organized by the churches twenty years ago. Certain people regret the inevitable political aspect which goes with any public manifestation, while others find it desirable. Be that as it may, it makes an Assembly extremely vulnerable.

As for the context of this Assembly, it has also given rise to another series of misunderstandings: there is much talk of the Third World, but what conception of it is applicable in Brazil and, more especially, to the province of Rio Grande do Sul? Many people have forgotten the title of one of the first books which described this enormous country, 36 times as large as the German Federal Republic. "Brazil, country of contrasts". Some people were preparing for their trip to Pôrto Alegre by reading revolutionary works, others were thinking of the economic problems and of the drought in the Northeast. Some people were already acquainted with the "Evangelical Church of Lutheran Confession in Brazil" because they have friends, relatives, pastors, and missionaries in it, and picture Brazil through the problems of the church. There are also those who were interested in the ecumenical aspect, and the fact that Brazil is one of the rare countries of the so-called Third World which has been Christian for more than four centuries but which has never had any direct contact with the consequences of the Reformation. Such a great diversity of interests brought panic in our church, which could scarcely recognize itself in all that was said and written about it.

You are perhaps surprised that I have not yet mentioned the essential problem, which some people would like to single out and restrict, but which for many people has a direct bearing on the witness of our faith. It should be stressed in this respect that the question of the political regime in Brazil was not of prime importance. It has often been said that this regime did not basically change between the revolution of March 1964 and the coup of November 1968. Even Act No. 5 of the Constitution did not arouse public opinion. But soon there was talk of tortures, repression, and the denial of basic human rights carried out by this regime in order to remain in power. The affair took on worldwide dimensions, with a press campaign well-organized against the so-called massacres of the Indians in Latin America. It was discovered, however, that too much importance had been given to this affair, although, at the same time, this campaign had a positive effect in that the situation of the Indians in Brazil was improved. This led our Brazilian brothers to jump to rather hasty conclusions in affirming that the case of the tortures was "also" just a trumped up affair!

In the "milieus" which were getting ready for Pôrto Alegre, people began to wonder what significance the holding of a world conference such as ours could have, in a country whose constitutional and democratic foundations had been shaken and where the liberties of the individual, and human rights were increasingly being denied. At all events, we had to make sure that our presence would not be interpreted as an indication that we supported the regime and we had to receive the necessary guarantees that the government would not try and exploit the situation. The responsible organs of the LWF always insisted on adhering to a set of conditions laid down for the normal conduct of the Assembly: right of entry for all participants, freedom of expression for everyone, exemption from censorship for the international press. It is significant that, starting with the meeting of the Executive Committee in Geneva (August 1968), the bodies in charge of the LWF, after a thorough examination of the situation, have always felt obliged to reaffirm their acceptance of the invitation from Brazil. Certain serious doubts were expressed but finally the desire to enter into dialog with the host church, and to assist it in its tasks, always prevailed. However, the basic question remained, that of the possible and necessary witness of this Assembly. By meeting in Latin America, the LWF wished to stress the importance of this continent and, at the same time, it wished to allow the context of the site to have an effect on the deliberations. The Youth Conference had also been prepared in this spirit, with some groups travelling through Spanish-speaking countries, and others through Brazil. All the delegates were encouraged to become acquainted with the situation on this continent. A bibliography was distributed and the church in Brazil wrote out more than 300 invitations for visits to its various parishes. But the more we became acquainted with the situation, and in particular the political, social and human situation, the more the problem of witness became essential and difficult. Would it be possible to speak both freely and critically? Was it courteous to attack the government of our host country? Are we mature enough to deal with this kind of uncomfortable situation? The last meeting of the Executive Committee in Vedbaek (December 1969) could not see any other possible alternative. In view of the theme we had chosen, we could not retreat. We had to go and try to find what constituted this witness, and already began by living our theme during this preparatory period.

Matters started deteriorating in Europe in March 1970. Several religious newspapers published critical articles, stating that the LWF was incapable of facing up to such a situation and that if it met in Brazil it would remain silent. Had it not already been proved in the past that the Lutherans were not always very clear as to their role vis-à-vis the state! Apart from several low blows of this kind, which were aimed for the most part at the confessional organization and did not really have any bearing on the questions posed by the Assembly, we were aware of a state of tension coming from two different points of departure, and which it was difficult to reconcile. On the one hand, it was thought that the only possible witness of the Assembly consisted in expressing our solidarity toward those who suffer in Brazil. Even the interest for the 800,000 Lutherans concentrated in the states of the South, where there is relatively little poverty and only a few political prisoners, could not counterbalance the political injustices committed in Brasilia, the police crimes in Rio, and the suffering in Recife. On the other hand, there were those for whom our going to Pôrto Alegre was not meant to have any immediate political consequences. The role of the Federation consisted in studying the theme which had been chosen at a universal level. To meet in Brazil signified, in particular, assisting the host church to play its part both politically and socially for which it had been ill prepared in the past.

The publication in the German "Evangelischer Pressedienst" of governmental and military documents received from the President of the Brazilian church had the effects of a bomb. This gesture was interpreted as the expression of a complete solidarity between the church and the regime. And, moreover, the press also reported that a growing number of Catholic churchmen and lay people were entering the ranks of the opposition and the resistance! It should be stated that certain people displayed a great naiveté in thinking that the majority of Brazilians were opposed to the regime. They had not taken into account the national feeling of this nation, expressed also in politics, not just in matters of football, and which reacts all the more violently when the criticism comes from outside and is voiced by foreigners.

In Italy, France, Germany, Holland, and Scandinavia, voices were heard demanding that, under these circumstances, the LWF should decline the Brazilian invitation, for fear that it would appear to condone the actions of those responsible for the tortures. To adhere to the decision was to prepare for a "confrontation" for the church itself in Brazil. The question had been put to those in charge of it more than a year ago, and their answer had been quite clear: we consider that the witness of the Assembly is basically situated at the world level. If it is sincere, biblical, and authentic, we are ready to meet the consequences at the national level.

Up to this period, the LWF had not received any request from any of the churches asking that the site of the Assembly be changed. Only one letter from the Ephorus of the Batak Church (Indonesia) inquired about the political situation in Brazil and the security of the participants. The number of reactions grew, however, due to the arousing of public opinion and the kidnapping of several diplomats. The weekend of May 1 and the week which followed, had been set aside for the meetings of three important delegations. At Arnoldshain (German Federal Republic), about forty Assembly participants reviewed the whole question and, like the National Committee of the LWF, wrote a letter to the President of the Federation, in which they expressed their anxiety and mentioned the eventual possibility of a change of site but, at the same time, indicated their wish to go to Pôrto Alegre, providing that a certain number of conditions were fulfilled. In Minneapolis, the United States delegation was also getting ready. Information concerning the tortures had taken a lot longer to be published. A cynical article criticizing the Lutherans had just appeared in *Christian Century*. On the eve of the meeting, President Nixon made his announcement about the sending of troops to Cambodia, and to some people, Brazil seemed rather remote. There was a certain malaise among the youth participants concerning Pôrto Alegre, and soon a student movement gathered together signatures for a manifesto asking that the LWF should not go there.

Next came the preparatory session of the Brazilian delegation in Blumenau (Santa Catarina), to which the church had invited those who would be responsible for interpreting the Assembly at the local and regional levels. This consultation was also important because the church was undergoing an experiment in unity, as, only two years previously, it was still divided into autonomous districts. The Arnoldshain declaration, published by the German delegation, was the object of lengthy discussions. Those at the heart of the Brazilian church are convinced that the advantages of the present regime far outweigh the disadvantages. They are particularly grateful to it for having put an end, in 1964, to political and economic stagnation, which could have led to a disaster. Of course, the return to democracy seemed to be taking its time, but since the government affirmed that its intentions were good, it was necessary to trust and support it. This was the only way to build up a strong and independent nation. As for the comparisons with the prewar Nazi situation, these were completely out of place. Shouldn't the country protect itself against terrorism! Faced with this conflict as to the analysis of the situation in Brazil, between the majority of representatives of the local church and a large proportion of those coming from abroad, the Pôrto Alegre Assembly looked like it had to be an Assembly of dialog or of confrontation, otherwise, it would lose its chance. In view of this confrontation, the conference presented a motion to the leaders of the church requesting that a commission of inquiry be set up to look into the question of the tortures.

A point of crystallization was soon to emerge and reveal the difficulties involved in this confrontation. After lengthy negotiations and with the request that invitations be sent to those concerned as soon as possible, the host church placed the President of the Republic at the head of its list, asking that an invitation should be addressed to him personally. The General Secretary of the Federation did not comply with this request, as he felt that the presence of the President would pose too many problems, and decided to refer the decision to the Officers, due to meet on May 20.

The Blumenau Consultation finished on May 7. Two days later, President Medici was due to be received in Pôrto Alegre. The Lutheran church, which has its headquarters in this town, took the necessary steps with a view to obtaining an audience with the President. The General Secretary of the LWF, who was also there at the time, indicated that he did not wish to be associated with such a step and took the opportunity that weekend of visiting congregations and inspecting the work carried out among the Indians in Tenanka Portella. Had he been present at such an audience, he would have had to express the criticisms being voiced in the ranks of the Federation, but which the Brazilian church did not yet feel ready to express itself. On the other hand, in discussing the plans of the LWF, he should normally have presented an invitation to the President. Moreover, this question was the subject of controversy, and was only due to be decided by the Officers on the 20th. The Brazilian delegation was composed, in fact, of representatives of the church and of Lutheran members of parliament. It had informed the President of its desire that he should be the guest of the LWF. On the eve of this audience, a deputy had expressed his joy to the

Regional Chamber that the LWF had chosen Pôrto Alegre as the Assembly site and also the wish that the President be invited to make a political speech there. To go from this, to saying that it was the church which had already invited the President to give a political speech, was a step which was quickly taken by both the local and international press. It is hardly surprising that this caused immediate and strong reactions from almost everywhere!

At their meeting in Geneva on May 20-21, the Officers of the Federation undertook a new analysis of the situation. There were three main questions under discussion: 1) A study of the facts relating to Brazil and the line of action to be taken by the Federation concerning them; 2) The conditions required for the free conduct of the Assembly; 3) What would be the consequences for the church in Brazil of a confrontation? The communiqué published at the end of this stormy session, said that the Officers of the LWF were aware of the risks being run because of the polarization of the points of view, but affirmed that since the external conditions for a free exchange had been given, the Federation could not avoid this dialog which might prove useful.

Those who criticized the choice of Assembly site, fearing that we would not be able to bring the necessary witness there, were evidently not satisfied, and continued to call for declarations condemning the Brazilian regime. But the greatest difficulty arose out of the fact that the decision of the Officers had not been unanimous. In fact, the First Vice-President of the Federation had disagreed with the rest of his colleagues and announced that he would not go to Pôrto Alegre. He became the focal point for an active minority in Northern Europe which was demanding that the site of the Assembly be changed. From this moment onwards, it was no longer isolated voices, but whole delegations, which saw in their refusal to go to Pôrto Alegre a way of protesting against the tortures.

In accordance with the decision taken by the Officers of the Federation, the General Secretary endeavored to explain the position of the Federation to the Executive Committee of the host church, meeting at Curitiba, Brazil on May 22-24. Once again, the difficult talks which ensued brought out a very sincere desire to understand the position of the sister churches and the wish to overcome all obstacles. On the question of the refusal to invite the President of the Republic, the Brazilians did not really want to give way, as they thought that since the Federation had accepted an invitation to Latin America, it should be willing to conform to the customs of this continent. Inviting a President is a necessary gesture of courtesy, without any political implications. The witness of the Assembly should take another form, especially as the church had not dreamed of requesting a political speech from the first person of the country. Under the present circumstances, and after the audience on May 9, it was perhaps not even necessary any more to present a formal invitation. Matters could be allowed to run their course; perhaps the President would not come, especially as during his previous visit to Pôrto Alegre, he had been informed of the reluctance on the part of certain delegations to go to Brazil.

During a telephone conversation with the President of the LWF on May 26, the General Secretary submitted to him an alternative proposal, drawn up by staff in Geneva. An invitation to President Medici ran the risk of compromising the conducting of the Assembly, especially as his presence there might incite protest demonstrations, which a military dictatorship could hardly allow. In order to keep open the possibility of a dialog, even with the government, we suggested that instead of requesting the President to come to Pôrto Alegre, a delegation from the Assembly should go to Brasilia, to explain the points of view expressed at the conference and to inform the government of its work. This suggestion, submitted to the Brazilian church in the form of a communiqué proposal, received a cold reception in Pôrto Alegre. President Gottschald, however, wished to consult with some of his colleagues in charge of the Assembly. On May 29, during another telephone conversation, this time with the General Secretary of the church, Geneva was informed that the President had gone to consult with various people and was asking for a respite of two days in order to be able to reply to two specific questions: 1) would the government consider it an insult not to be invited; 2) would the host church agree to disregard polite customs and not insist on inviting the President? Meanwhile, telephone messages were flying between Geneva, Stockholm, Copenhagen, Helsinki, Hanover, Stuttgart, New York, and Minneapolis. A growing number of delegates seemed to have decided not to attend. The question of whether an Assembly, which was reduced in size, could make decisions, which would be valid for the whole of the Lutheran world, was received from East Berlin. However, President Schiotz was convinced that if the Brazilian church maintained its invitation, we were not in a position to gainsay it. On May 30, President Gottschald reported on the results of his consultations. The government would not be represented at the Assembly, but the church could not simply give way on the principle of the invitation, although it wished to do all in its power to save the Assembly. Was it already too late? . . . President Schiotz decided that Pôrto Alegre should still remain the Assembly site, especially as a telegram received from the Brazilian youth delegation, and those in charge of it, urgently requested us not to shun the difficulties.

On Sunday, May 31, most of the Swedish delegation decided, nevertheless, to boycott Pôrto Alegre, and some of them encouraged others to do likewise. It requested us to meet somewhere else and proposed Stockholm; others, in Germany, suggested that we hold a smaller Assembly in Geneva. The communiqué of June 1 should be viewed as a last attempt, not at forcing the hands of those who were still expressing doubts and warnings, but at taking seriously the demands of the theme of the Assembly and the wishes of the host church. The fact that it was published in Brazil in a shortened form, and only mentioned that the President could not be invited, was interpreted there as a challenge and insult to the nation. This caused a telegram of protest to be received from President Gottschald, after a stormy visit of representatives of the church to the governor and to the Legislature of Rio Grande do Sul.

During our last telephone conversation, President Gottschald himself wondered if, under the present conditions, an Assembly could still be meaningful. The conditions laid down by the Executive Committee and Officers of the LWF could not be fulfilled: the church was so indignant that it had taken up an uncompromising and partisan attitude towards its government, so that it was no longer in a position to hold a dialog. Each side would only have provoked the other, and there did not seem to be adequate awareness of the risks. By publicly renewing its invitation to the President of the Republic, against the wishes of the Federation, the latter was no longer, in fact, master of its own Assembly. And, furthermore, the growing number of delegations which were refusing to attend, ran the risk of jeopardizing the size of the Assembly and compromising its decisions.

After dilemma, came deadlock! Only a brutal decision could avert disaster. It was taken, once again, after numerous telephone conversations during the night, and officially made public on June 5.

Do not think that we did not weigh all the risks and that we were not conscious of the deep wounds we were inflicting on the church in Brazil, which, after having prepared itself in all seriousness and even been open to the criticism and assistance of its brothers in other continents, perhaps took refuge at least for a short time, in a nationalistic, isolationist position! Since then, we found ourselves in the paradoxical situation in which the compass needle has passed from the heavy pressure against Pôrto Alegre, with the defections of several delegations, to a movement which may even be stronger still, of protest against Evian, but where there is almost maximum attendance. So, here we are then, not in the haven of joy (Pôrto Alegre), but in a haven, said to be peaceful (Evian), and now it's your turn!

May I, before concluding, add a few personal remarks: 1) Evian is not a place of refuge. We chose it because it was the only town which could receive us at such short notice, and which was able to offer us 600 beds. We should not have been able to hold either a confrontation or a dialog in Pôrto Alegre, due to polarization of points of view, which could not have been expressed there. You have brought with you to Evian all the knowledge and anxiety of the Latin American context, which you have developed during these two years of preparation. We are not beginning again at zero. No, we are continuing research which, at all events, extended far beyond the frontiers of Brazil.

2) The dialog with the Brazilian church will not really be able to take place here, and I regret this very much. It is up to us to find ways and means of continuing it after Evian. In order to prepare ourselves, let us endeavor, while we are here, to listen to each other, before pronouncing judgment on ourselves.

Let us learn what is meant by a dialog, which should express a common witness. This will also make us reflect again on the role which criticism can and should play in the church. Some would like to throttle it in order to allow only their own point of view. Others deliberately take advantage of it, in order to cause confusion. The experience of these last few months has made some people anxious about the future of the LWF. We should not dramatize events. If our communion is authentic, it will emerge purified, and fortified, and its wounds will heal over quickly. Perhaps we should first of all pay more attention to certain of the requirements of the communion of our faith, and of its expression in the world. Above all, let us not be afraid of acting freely, in the way in which Luther has described so beautifully, and of which he has given us such striking examples; but let us not forget charity.

3) The aims of the LWF are not only situated at a theological level, but also at the existential level of the lives of our churches in the world. The most difficult problem for us at the present time is that of the political witness of the church. Was it a theological consideration which forced us to change the Assembly site from Pôrto Alegre? It is obvious that in the future we shall not choose an Assembly site simply because a certain political regime is liberal or well-disposed toward us; but if the aim of an Assembly is not political, what kind of a role should it play in this field in order to remain faithful to the demands of the faith? Have we only come up against problems of method and tactics, or have we also touched upon one of substance? What should our witness be in a situation of world crisis, and how can we express our solidarity with the victims of injustice? How should we assess a situation? By taking as our starting point an extreme awareness of the situation, when viewed from the outside, and censored information and an excessive form of conditioning within it . . . ?

4) Finally, it is obvious that we should also reexamine our method of working, and the way in which we conceive and organize a world assembly. May our experience also prove useful to other ecumenical bodies which are seeking the same solutions.

But let us not enumerate too many questions. Let us not lose time in considering the faults which have been committed for fear that we shall no longer be able to look at the way we are going and face up to the responsibilities which we must assume. I find it very encouraging that this Assembly has aroused so much interest, almost everywhere. However, the decisive element is the fact that never before has one of our Assemblies been supported by so many prayers. This could not have been in vain.

Concern was expressed from the floor that much of the information contained in this report had not been made available prior to the decision to change the site. Regret was expressed that the site had been changed. Evian does not provide the context for learning and discussing the questions with which the LWF is confronted in the Third World. These questions are not only social, political, and economic, but also questions related to theology, ecumenism and evangelism. The LWF must soon "go into the Third World".

b) Mr. Reinhard Gleisner (Chile) requested permission as a participant in the World Encounter of Lutheran Youth to read the following statement prepared by this conference:

Statement: Change of the Assembly Site

The site of the Fifth Assembly of the Lutheran World Federation has been moved from Pôrto Alegre to Evian, France. It is of no use to discuss whether it was a right or a wrong decision, but it is important to recognize the implications of the decisions for the LWF, its member churches and the Assembly itself. Without a clear awareness of the complicity of the North Atlantic countries in the creation and maintenance of the situation of injustice in Brazil and throughout the Third World, our criticism is empty and simply serves to obscure the real issues.

The decision illustrates several facts about the structure and decision-making process of the LWF.

1. First of all, there was a lack of participation by the Third World people in the making of the decision: it was decided by European and US church leaders, a process which denied participation to most of the people of member churches. This was a decision reflecting the sources of power in an LWF structure whose primary economic and political support is secured in a continuing North Atlantic ecclesiastical colonialism.

2. Secondly, it illustrates LWF's fear to deal with the social and political issues of the world in which it operates. The LWF refuses to discuss politics, including and especially the political situation in Brazil, preferring rather an abstract safe theological discussion. The LWF did not seem to understand that a thorough discussion on these issues is necessary to understand the prospects, implications and consequences of an Assembly in Pôrto Alegre.

3. Thirdly, the lack of information dissemination, by LWF member churches about all the issues involved in the decision demonstrates LWF's desire to hold an assembly in silence.

117

The Evangelical Church of Lutheran Confession in Brazil, as well as the LWF, refused to recognize its political responsibilities, by refusing to acknowledge the credibility of the reports of torture in Brazil and by its lack of criticism of the military regime. There was a lack of discussion of real issues among a large group of the members of the church.

The situation created by the move is a very bad one, but it would not have occurred if:

1. The LWF and its member churches had recognized their political responsibility. The individualistic ethic, because of a misunderstanding of the doctrine of the two kingdoms, has not allowed the church to engage in political and social problems. The issue is not that the church attempts to gain political power but that it recognizes that it already possesses that power.

2. That power had been wielded to fight for humanization and justice for the poor and oppressed against all economic and political repressive systems, for example: to exert political pressure to change the system that results in torture of political prisoners in Brazil: to move against US genocide in South East Asia: to support the liberation movements in Mozambique, Portuguese Angola, and Portuguese Guinea: to work for the eradication of the system of apartheid in South Africa: racism in USA: institutional violence against foreign migrant workers in Europe: and trade and customs systems created by the rich world, that probably kill more people than the other situations mentioned.

3. The church had been committed to the creation of true community and participatory democracy that does not deny any part of that community.

We are in Evian. We must resist the temptation to polarize the Assembly by debating the merits of the decision to move, but rather make this Assembly a working Assembly. Because we are removed from the Third World it will be doubly hard to feel the urgency of their problems, but despite the fact of our removal from the Third World context, we are still confronted by those issues, and must reconstruct and revitalize the LWF in the light of the urgency of this situation. Furthermore, we demand that, if a next assembly is held, it must be held in the Third World.

c) Dean Kastlund (Sweden), Vice-Chairman of the Commission on Latin America, requested permission to read a statement prepared by the Commission on Latin America at its recent meeting in St. Louis:

Statement of the Commission on Latin America to the Fifth Assembly of the Lutheran World Federation at Evian-les-Bains, France.

At Hanover in 1952, the Second Assembly of the LWF called into existence the Committee on Latin America and after the Fourth Assembly in Helsinki it became a Commission. At this Fifth Assembly it will cease to exist as an autonomous agency of the LWF and become part of a new Department of Church Cooperation.

It had been our expectation that 18 years of history would culminate in Pôrto Alegre, Brazil, thus according to Latin America—and thereby to the "two-thirds world"—that attention and significance which it so justly deserves.

Our Commission had a small part in the proposed plans for Pôrto Alegre but owing to the rapidity with which events developed, no voice in the decision to withdraw from Brazil. Without presuming to apportion blame, which very many of us share, we feel that damage has been done to the fabric of our Lutheran fellowship which may require years to repair. Two things are needful now: one, that every effort be made by all of us to heal the wounds in our ecumenical body and, two, that the tragic sequence of events be prevented, if humanly possible, from ever being repeated.

Therefore we offer the following recommendations:

1. That the Officers, the Executive Committee, the staff—and especially the new Committee on Latin America—of the LWF be instructed to seek a full restoration of fellowship with the Evangelical Church of Lutheran Confession in Brazil and give particular attention to making amends to our brethren in Brazil and throughout Latin America wherever the rich benefits of fellowship to be derived from the Pôrto Alegre Assembly had been anticipated, especially through visitations, conferences, etc.

2. That steps be taken to lay down specific guidelines with respect to the nature and purpose of LWF assemblies, including a clear delineation of duties and responsibilities in planning and preparation. The Commission on Latin America does not wish to prejudge the issue but simply stresses the importance of a better understanding of the theological and political presuppositions in choosing a location and arranging the program.

President Schiotz referred the recommendations to the new Executive Committee.

d) The General Secretary read a statement prepared by the Executive Committee at its meeting in Evian, July 10-12:

Statement of the Executive Committee Meeting in Evian, July 10-12

The Executive Committee expresses its deep gratitude to the Evangelical Church of Lutheran Confession in Brazil for the extensive preparations made to entertain the Fifth Assembly of the Lutheran World Federation. We have a sympathetic understanding for the disappointment experienced by the church at the decision to relocate the Assembly, and indeed we share in the disappointment. It had been our expectation to come to Pôrto Alegre, Brazil, thus according to Latin America and thereby to the so-called Third World, the attention and significance which it so justly deserves. According to the authorization given by the Executive Committee at previous meetings the Officers made their decision in good faith amid rapid and complex developments. We express our appreciation to the Officers and staff for expending themselves tirelessly under exceedingly difficult circumstances.

We recommend that the new Executive Committee consider guidelines on the nature and purpose of LWF assemblies, including the presuppositions in choosing a location and arranging the program. We also recommend that the Executive Committee explore the means for encouraging member churches to give loyal support to decisions reached according to the constituted order of the Federation. Important decisions should not be changed under pressure from individual churches, when the majority of the member churches cannot be consulted.

It was received as information.

e) Professor Wingren (Sweden) requested the Assembly not to look to the past but to the future, suggesting that Dom Helder Camara be proposed to the Nobel Prize Committee for the Nobel Peace Prize. The President proposed that this suggestion be referred to the Resolutions Committee.

f) Criticism was raised from the floor concerning the information process within the LWF and concerning alleged censorship of the LWF News Services. Does the information practice of the LWF reflect an apolitical stance, a false interpretation of the doctrine of the two kingdoms, and a concern for self-preservation by the LWF? The questions were raised: 1) whether there will again be censorship of LWF information and 2) when there will finally be a political theology in the LWF.

The General Secretary responded that in his opinion there was no censorship in the LWF and that only in the last six weeks to two months had he asked to see all information on Brazil before it was released. Otherwise the Information Office of the LWF had complete freedom. The limited means of the Information Office prevented providing more complete information. If the member churches were prepared to double the budget of the Information Office, the LWF might be in a position to meet this request for better information.

Plenary III
Tuesday evening
July 14, 1970 and
Wednesday morning
July 15, 1970.

g) The continuing debate centered on the following issues:

1. It was stated that the LWF in not going to Pôrto Alegre had lost a great opportunity for witness in the Brazilian situation. Evian, a French resort, was not the place for dealing with those social and economic questions to be faced by an LWF assembly at this time. By not going to Brazil, the LWF had forced the Evangelical Church of Lutheran Confession in Brazil into solidarity with the Brazilian government. This, however, was challenged by those who maintained that it was not at all clear whether the LWF would have had anything to say at all to the specific questions raised by Brazil. The preparatory documents for Section III were criticized as not being substantive and being too conservative.

2. Fear was expressed that the consequence of the LWF's decision might be that in the future one could only meet in countries where righteousness and justice prevailed. Does not the doctrine of justification demand that we be willing to go into each and every situation?

3. Criticisms were also raised concerning the way in which the decision had been reached. Sufficient information was not provided to the churches. Information, however, is not the sole question, since there is always the problem of interpreting information—effective decisions must be made. Specific criticism was directed to those delegations who had announced their decision not to attend the Assembly at Pôrto Alegre.

4. Disappointment was expressed that the decision to hold the Assembly in the Third World had been frustrated by western churches. There was little respect for the opinions of the churches in the Third World and no consultation with them. The younger churches after achieving their independence discovered that the western churches, being larger and having greater financial resources, were

the dominant churches in the LWF. "Is the LWF not another form of domination?"

The question was raised as to whether a real attempt had been made to find an alternate site in Latin America. Not responding directly to this question, the president pointed out that assemblies were held at the invitations of member churches and suggested that there might be a caucus of representatives of churches in the Third World which might recommend to the new Executive Committee proposals for a site for the next assembly.

5. Other delegates supported the Officers in the difficult decision that they were forced to take.

6. There was a call to look to the present challenge of this Assembly and the suggestion was made that a strong statement on human rights and torture should be forthcoming. Criticism, however, was directed to the suggestion by Professor Wingren (cf. 7e) that Dom Helder Camara be proposed for the Nobel Peace Prize. The greatest honor that the LWF could have bestowed on Archbishop Camara would have been to go to Brazil and speak a clear word. Since this was not assured other delegates were also against going to Brazil, feeling that the LWF could not make a witness in that situation. The task was now to speak such a clear word.

7. The question of the relation of politics and religion was posed. On the one hand, individual Christians as citizens have the right and duty to engage in politics, but the church and a religious organization like the LWF did not have a political mandate. Others held that the church had to speak on human rights on the basis of the word of God. There was the necessity for enunciating a "political theology" which would explicate the doctrine of the two kingdoms in a correct manner.

8. Attention should be given to future relations with the Lutheran church in Brazil. Positive steps should be taken to overcome the alienation that has been caused by the decision not to go to Pôrto Alegre.

h) The President reminded the plenary that there was limited time for continuing the debate. Therefore a formal motion to close debate after hearing from the Latin American representatives was passed.

i) The following representatives from Latin America were given the floor.

1. President Heinz Joachim Held (Official Visitor, Argentina) pointed

out the lack of trust which had developed between the LWF and the Brazilian church and the lack of communication. "We find ourselves in a solidarity of helplessness." He questioned whether the appeal to the LWF by the western churches to call off the Assembly in Brazil was an effectual political witness.

2. Pastor Manuel de Mello (Observer-Consultant, Pentecostal Church "Brazil para Cristo", Sao Paulo) expressed the regret of Protestants of Brazil and stated that the arguments used in cancelling the Assembly in Brazil were not convincing. He referred to Luther's courage in going to Worms, and although respecting the decision of the LWF Executive Committee, expressed his disappointment concerning it, pointing out that the decision had been damaging to the whole Protestant movement in Latin America.

3. President Karl Gottschald (Adviser, ECLCB) stated that he had not desired to speak, but had been requested to do so. He did not wish to prolong the controversy and pointed to the communion service of that morning. He wished, however, to make two points for correction and clarification of remarks of the General Secretary in his report. He wished to point out that a commission of the church on social and political affairs had already been constituted in December 1968 and not just after the Assembly preparation conference in Blumenau in May 1970. As to the question of the invitation to the President of Brazil, the church had acted in good faith in response to a specific request from the General Secretariat of the LWF in February 1970 to the church in Brazil to provide a list of possible invitees including the rector of the university and high government officials.

He then read a statement of the Council of the ECLCB on the decision of the LWF Officers to cancel the Pôrto Alegre Assembly:

Statement of the Council of the Evangelical Church of Lutheran Confession in Brazil regarding the change of location of the Fifth General Assembly of the Lutheran World Federation

The relocation at short notice of the Fifth General Assembly of the LWF, a few weeks before its planned meeting in Pôrto Alegre, was received with deep regret and with displeasure by the ECLCB and by the Brazilian public. The question regarding the meaning and purpose of a General Assembly of the LWF and in connection with it the question regarding the presuppositions of Christian witness in the world generally, are being asked more urgently than before and not only in church circles. In addition to this, the time and the form of the cancellation, as it appeared in the press, has had an extremely negative effect in that much personal involvement and cooperation, great expectations, and already accomplished effort were disappointed.

There are several reasons for the inability to understand the sudden decision of the LWF. The preconditions which existed at the time of the acceptance of the ECLCB's invitation on the part of the LWF have not basically changed in the meantime. This holds true in view of both the political conditions in Brazil as well as the readiness of the host church to accept the participants of the meeting and to eliminate as far as possible any obstacles which might arise. It should be expressly emphasized that no kind of pressure or influence has been exercised by the governmental agencies on the decisions and plans of the ECLCB. Therefore the thought never occurred to the host church that the Assembly might be misused as a political platform by any partisan political group.

The LWF was informed early enough and repeatedly about the political and other conditions in Brazil. The LWF did not inform us of the objections to Pôrto Alegre as the site of the meeting until a few weeks before its cancellation. The reason for the sudden change in the mood of many member churches and even of the staff of the LWF itself, we believe is chiefly because of tendentious news items which recently aroused the international public about the existence of deplorable conditions in our country. Aside from the question as to what extent this was a case of proper reporting and to what extent it was distorted reporting, two aspects of the churches' reaction to these reports remain questionable to us.

1. If the church feels itself called upon to fulfill its task of political guardianship, knowledge of the matter and an unprejudiced attitude are two prerequisites which are absolutely necessary. The ECLCB regrets that Lutheran churches and groups within them trusted too little; that not enough was done to procure the proper information when needed on the spot, at any rate from the proper authorities; and that prejudice took the place of balance of judgment.

2. Beyond this, we ask the fundamental question: Is it imperative that certain political and social conditions must be met before a church can give its witness in a particular place? Does not the Assembly of the LWF, through the change of site, get just the political character which it should not have?

The Assembly of the LWF became an instrument of political tendencies at the moment in which the question regarding the location was isolated from the watchword "Sent into the World", and decided in accordance with the laws of political expediency. In our opinion, Christian witness cannot be given in avoiding political and human conflicts, even when this is meant to be a sign or when it happens out of tactical reasons.

The ECLCB furthermore cannot avoid the impression that the objectives of a General Assembly of the LWF are determined differently according to the site. The points of view which were decisive for the choice of earlier sites show that apparently the LWF operates in a way incommensurate with the character of a General Assembly with two kinds of criteria—a fact which radically breaks away from the credibility and freedom of the church of Jesus Christ.

Finally, we would like especially to ask about the role which the Lutheran press offices in Geneva played in the debate over the meeting site during the final weeks. Unnecessary problems were created by news reports which can be shown to be distorted. To what extent were such reports already sent out by the press office in Geneva? The lack of an objective press is, in the opinion of the ECLCB, to no small extent responsible for the harm which has been caused the ECLCB and the LWF itself as a result of the change in location of the Assembly.

It follows from what has been said that our church, toward which insufficient trust has been extended, will not be represented at Evian in the way foreseen. Too much trust has been gambled away for us to be able to justify before our congregations, before the other churches in Brazil, and before the public, the appearance as though nothing had happened. Since we are of the opinion that the church must also bear tensions and human mistakes, from which we do not seek to absolve ourselves herewith, we are not withdrawing from the work. Christian cooperation must be possible also in times of inner-church crises. We believe that the LWF must now become clear about what is its actual task and which working methods correspond to this task.

Pôrto Alegre, July 1970

> The Council of the
> Evangelical Church of
> Lutheran Confession in Brazil

j) A point of order was raised requesting the chair to permit youth representatives from Brazil to respond to President Gottschald. This request was rejected as not having been included in the motion to close debate which had been adopted.

k) President Schiotz allowed the following amended motion—presented in unamended form earlier in the debate—to be made and seconded:

RESOLVED: The Assembly endorses the judgment that "the change of location has forfeited a great opportunity" and urges that in future opportunities be sought to make good what may have been lost.

This resolution was referred to the Policy and Reference Committee

l) The President reported that the Executive Committee had appointed an ad hoc committee consisting of the following persons: Professors T. Rendtorff and K. Rajaratnam, Doctors C. Thomas, C. Walther and I. Asheim, with Professor H. E. Tödt as adviser, to bring in a report at this time. Professor Rajaratnam in his introductory remarks stated this report must be seen in the context of the Lutheran churches historic failure to identify themselves with situations arising out of political, economic, and social exploitation. He then presented the following report:

Introduction

"Sent into the World" is the theme of the Fifth Assembly of the Lutheran World Federation. Yet the Assembly suddenly finds itself meeting in a place which seems to be a symbolic contradiction to the theme. Questions are being asked, facts given and interpreted in various ways, and even in some instances the finger of blame has been pointed. It therefore is imperative that this Assembly be clear on the issue which has moved us from Pôrto Alegre to Evian.

The Issue

What then is the issue? The issue facing this Assembly is that of our response to a time of crisis which is symbolized by increasing violation of human rights. The issue came into focus by Brazil but is certainly not only Brazil or a particular form of government since no government is perfectly just. We acknowledge that each of us views the problem of human rights from a different perspective. But because of our common humanity it is necessary that we openly and freely discuss the various ways in which we see this issue so that efforts may be derived to promote our common cause of justice. The main question is: Can Christians individually and corporately face social crises with integrity? Furthermore, can we express our solidarity with our fellow human beings wherever they may suffer?

We confess that all too many times we have been indecisive about our

126

task when clarity has been demanded. This has been historically true when the matter of human rights has been at stake. In those instances, such as South-West Africa, where we have acted the results have been apparent. Where we have been indecisive we have failed. In this respect we share responsibility for failure as individual Christians, as churches, and as common ecumenical agencies.

The guilt we experience today, both corporately and individually, is that of those who have been confronted by the demands of the living Lord but have failed to respond. We have not recognized that just as nations are interdependent so our churches are dependent on one another. Therefore, when one suffers all suffer. In facing problems we have been far too concerned with strategies and tactics and not enough concerned with the principle of justice. The church responds in its unique way only as it sees the issues in the context of its total life—namely worship, theological reflection, ethical decision-making, and social action.

The Declaration

Therefore, we who proclaim God in Christ for all men, this day assembled in Evian do make the following declaration:

1. We turn to Almighty God in prayer as the church has always done in times of crisis, seeking first his forgiveness for our failures and secondly, strength to meet with courage the crises of the day.
2. We recognize that we are a pilgrim people in but not of this world. The Lord, who demands our loyalty, calls us to live the Christian style of life with integrity, and to assume the risks this entails. Our identity as a church and as a people rests not where we live but in whom we live.
3. We ask the forgiveness of all our brothers in the world whom we have offended in many situations by seeking that which is expedient before that which is just.
4. We pledge our corporate and individual efforts to strive for the establishment of human rights and dignity for all men recognizing that in so doing we have no easy or simple answer amidst the painful ambiguities of the day.
5. We rejoice that we have been freed by him so that we can now freely assume the burdens of others.

Recommendation

That Sections I, II, and III in their deliberations consider this document and be prepared to report to the Assembly proposals designed to implement the intent of this paper.

The Assembly was asked whether it was willing to receive the report of this ad hoc committee. Receiving the report would not imply approval. A motion was made, seconded, and adopted:

1. that the report be received;

2. that the recommendations be referred to the three Assembly Sections "to implement the intent of this paper".

(8) Lecture by Professor Heinz Eduard Tödt: "Creative Discipleship in the Contemporary World Crisis" (see pp. 31-42).

Without further discussion the lecture was referred to the three Assembly Sections as resource material.

(9) Steering Committees for the Sections

In adopting the Rules of Procedure, provision had been made for Section Steering Committees. These were appointed.

(10) Ad Hoc Committee on Lutheran/Reformed Relations

The Executive Committee recommended the appointment of a special ad hoc committee, "to study the report of the Lutheran/Reformed Joint Committee and submit its report to the Assembly as information, for transmission to the churches". The motion to do so was made, seconded, and adopted.

Plenary IV
Wednesday evening
July 15, 1970

(11) Recognition of Local Guests

The General Secretary introduced special guests from the Roman Catholic Church in Evian and expressed his gratitude for the accommodations which had been made available to the Assembly by their institutions.

(12) Greetings from Ecumenical Guests

The following ecumenical guests brought greetings to the Assembly:

a) the Rt. Rev. Neil Russell, Assistant Bishop of Edinburgh, representing the Anglican Communion and the Archbishop of Canterbury,

b) Professor Wilhelm Niesel, President of the World Alliance of Reformed Churches.

(13) Lecture by Professor Kent Knutson: "The Response of the Lutheran Churches to the Roman Catholic Church and Theology Today" (see pp. 43-53).

(14) Lecture by Cardinal Jan Willebrands: "Sent into the World" (see pp. 54-65).

Plenary V
Friday afternoon
July 17, 1970

(15) Second Report of the Credentials Committee (see item 51 for Final Report).

(16) First Report of the Minutes Committee

The minutes were approved as presented.

(17) The President announced that word had just been received of the death of Dr. D. T. Niles, one of the presidents of the World Council of Churches. Mr. K. D. Benjamin (India) and Bishop H. Lilje (Federal Republic of Germany) expressed words of deep appreciation for the life and work of Dr. Niles to the whole ecumenical movement.

(18) Presentation of Further Ecumenical Guests

a) Professor Nikos Nissiotis, Associate General Secretary of the World Council of Churches,

b) The Rt. Rev. Metropolitan Emilianos Timiades, Representative of His Holiness, the Ecumenical Patriarch of Constantinople,

c) Archpriest P. Sokolovski, representing Metropolitan Poeman of the Krutizi and of the Kolomna, successor of Patriarch Alexei of Moscow,

d) The Rev. Manuel de Mello of the Pentecostal Church "Brazil para Cristo".

(19) Executive Committee Report and Recommendations

The General Secretary introduced the Executive Committee Report and Recommendations. Questions and comments from the floor centered on the following questions:

a) Interconfessional Dialog with the Roman Catholic Church

The question was raised as to why the Joint Commission on the Theology of Marriage and the Problem of Mixed Marriages had not come into being. In response, it was pointed out that because the

Roman Catholic Church itself had not until recently clarified its own position it would not be possible to begin conversations until later this year. In the meantime, preparations had been made by the LWF and the World Alliance of Reformed Churches for common discussion with the Roman Catholic Church on this point.

b) The relations to the Lutheran Church—Missouri Synod and other non-member Lutheran churches

The question was raised as to why the Missouri Synod had not responded positively as yet to the amendments of the LWF constitution made at Helsinki and as to what the relations of the LWF were to other nonmember Lutheran churches.

Vice-President Dr. Theodore F. Nickel of the Lutheran Church—Missouri Synod responded that at its last convention the Missouri Synod had found itself unable, in part because of the priority of the question of fellowship with the ALC and in part for financial reasons, to act positively on the recommendation of the church's Commission on Theology and Church Relations that application for membership in the LWF be made. The question would undoubtedly be raised again at the convention in 1971. He mentioned that the India Evangelical Lutheran Church, a Missouri Synod-related church, had become a member of the LWF and that the Lutheran Church—Missouri Synod had opened the door for this application.

President Max Lohe of the Lutheran Church of Australia mentioned that the Commission on Theology of his church had not yet seriously considered the question of fellowship relations with Lutheran churches outside Australia or LWF membership.

c) The New LWF Structure

In response to questions the President stated that the structure had been adopted by the Executive Committee on authority of the Helsinki Assembly and that any proposals for change could be submitted to the Business Committee and/or the PRC. The General Secretary stated that as to ecumenical cooperation, no special department was envisaged, but this was intended as a dimension of the work of all three new commissions and departments. The division into three departments was based chiefly on practical considerations. The new Commission on Studies was to incorporate the concerns of the previous study units, and was to set priorities, emphasis being placed on an interdisciplinary approach to all study questions. As to the advisability of establishing a special desk in the Department of Studies to deal with the concerns of the young generation, it was important to bring youth into all the work of the Federation. The question of the desirability of having area desks staffed by persons from the area concerned would be referred to the General Secretary and the new Executive Committee.

d) Development Study

A question was raised concerning the kind of "basic discussions regarding development" in which the LWF is involved. The Director of the Department of World Service responded that the Department had been in permanent contact with agencies conducting studies like the UNO, FAO, and UNESCO and the Development Commission of the International Council of Voluntary Agencies and hopes to deepen its study in the light of political and social concerns raised.

e) The Responsibility of the LWF for Peace and European Security

This question was to be brought to the attention of the leadership of Section III.

(20) First Report of the Business Committee

a) The Business Committee defined its role and relationship to other Assembly Committees in accordance with the adopted Rules of Procedure.

Received as information.

b) The resolution concerning the change of Assembly site (cf. item 7k) was to be referred to the Resolutions Committee.

Received as information.

c) Consideration was given to the proposal of delegates L. Stoll (FRG) and H. Göldner (FRG) on constitutional amendments. The Business Committee appointed a subcommittee to study this proposal.

d) The Business Committee had been informed that Miss Lyimo (Tanzania) was leaving Evian and recommended that delegate Andrej Ziak (Czechoslovakia) replace her on the Credentials and Elections Committee. Adopted.

(21) Discussion of Professor Tödt's lecture, "Creative Discipleship in the Contemporary World Crisis" (see pp. 31-42).

a) Professor Tödt was asked if he was not too optimistic concerning the possibility of changing the priorities within the western nations, since the large industrial corporations driven by competition and the profit motive seemed to be incapable of change and should be abolished. Professor Tödt responded that his view was perhaps more pessimistic than optimistic, but the vital question was how to find the real forces in securing basic change. The power structure was itself under threat and world society itself was endangered by the new technological achievements which could no longer be controlled.

b) Asked whether the character of this Assembly had encouraged him as to the role of the church, he responded that he was shocked by how little courage was shown to describe clearly and sharply the situation we face. Nevertheless, he would add that the process of rethinking and relearning takes time, and this gives him reason for hope. In a sense, this Assembly was "prehistoric" in that the forms of its work, its structure and the time allowed did not provide for getting deeply enough into the theological questions.

c) Was the statement that the problem facing man was no longer how to find a gracious God but rather was the difficulty of man in relation to his neighbor and his place in the universe perhaps a Western view that is not shared by the East or South? Professor Tödt responded that this question is really universal, although it is put in different ways in different continents.

d) Professor Tödt was questioned concerning his understanding of the Lutheran churches' responsibility, for identifying with the Lutheran churches in the Third World and, for expressing solidarity with the largely nonchristian masses that live in hunger and injustice. In responding he asked: Is the Christian message and the ethical criteria of Christianity understandable for all men or only understandable on the suppositions of faith? In his view, the Sermon on the Mount can be understood by all men, it addresses itself to reason, not as it is, but as it could be at its deepest levels, calling reason to its own better possibilities. There is such a thing as scientific reason which is separated from love, becoming unreasonable in itself. This means that Christian faith and action is to be so formulated that it leads to cooperation with persons who are completely secular.

e) A comment was made regarding the problem faced by the younger churches in Asia and Africa. The churches in these lands are making every effort to introduce stewardship, while the buying power of the members decreases because of the structure of the world market. The appeal was made to the mission societies, boards, and churches, to change their policy to see that financial help is not tied to the supplying of western personnel. In response Professor Tödt emphasized how much there was still to learn in this whole question. Obviously, new structures will be necessary.

(22) Second Report of the Minutes Committee

The minutes were approved as presented.

(23) Open Hearing on the Work of the General Secretariat

The General Secretary gave a short introduction to the various units connected with the work of the General Secretariat, pointing out that several of these would be redistributed in the new structure.

a) Bishop Wölber (FRG), read a proposed resolution whose purpose was to set the theological accents of the work of the LWF. This was referred to the Resolutions Committee.

b) Community Development Service

A question was raised concerning the fact that such a large percentage of the work of CDS was supported by agencies in only two countries, the Federal Republic of Germany (FRG) and Sweden. Why were funds from the United States not forthcoming for this important work? In response, the Director of the Department of World Service and Mr. Bernard Confer, Executive Secretary of Lutheran World Relief, emphasized that funds from the United States were given chiefly on an undesignated basis for the total work of the Federation.

The Director stated that the CDS program of the LWF works in close coordination with the World Council of Churches.

c) Scholarship and Exchange Program

A question was raised concerning the limitation of the LWF program to member churches and the cooperation with the World Council of Churches. In response, the Secretary of the Scholarship and Exchange Program emphasized that close cooperation did exist with the WCC. The program of the WCC is aimed at exchange between denominations, whereas the program of the LWF was primarily between member churches.

d) The New LWF Structure

In response to a question as to whether centralization or decentralization was the aim of the new structure, the General Secretary replied that these terms did not apply since the aim was greater coordination.

The aim of the new structure was to prevent institutionalization of concerns and provide greater flexibility in the work.

Concerning the place and importance of education within the new structure, the director-elect of the new Department of Studies, pointed out that the new Commission on Studies would have to describe carefully the terms of reference for work in this field and that education should be seen in a broader context, including theological education and the question of educational reform.

As to the financing of the work of the Federation, the Treasurer pointed out that whereas the total program of the Federation jumped from 3.2 million dollars in 1963 to 8.2 in 1970 (an almost threefold increase), staff had only increased by 40%.

e) Youth and Student Work

Reference was made to the suggestion that a youth and student desk be established at the LWF headquarters. It was pointed out that the World Encounter of Lutheran Youth had refrained from requesting a special youth desk, but instead requested places for youth in the whole decision-making process of the LWF.

f) Interconfessional Dialog

Any resolution regarding the continuation of the dialog between the LWF and the Roman Catholic Church should be submitted through the proper channels.

g) International Affairs

Concerning the function of the Executive Committee's Subcommittee on International Affairs, the General Secretary replied that the subcommittee had met each time the Executive Committee had met and that there had been various proposals for closer cooperation with the CCIA.

(24) Second Report of the Business Committee

a) In response to the request of delegates Stoll and Göldner (cf. item 20c), "Amendment of the Constitution", the Business Committee suggested that a subcommittee be appointed to discuss the proposed amendment and come with a recommendation at a later time (cf. item 61).

Received as information.

b) Proposal for a new Agenda Item, Amendment to the Constitution

The Business Committee has received from the Nominations Committee a recommendation that the constitution be amended to have 22 members of the Executive Committee (plus the President) rather than the 19 members (plus the President) now provided, and that these three additional members be assigned one each to the areas, Africa, Asia, and Latin America.

The Business Committee

RECOMMENDED: That to the agenda be added the point: "Amendment of the Constitution", and submits the following amendment:

In the constitution, Article VIII, entitled "Executive Committee", point 1 which now reads: "Each Assembly shall elect nineteen persons who with the President shall constitute the Executive Committee of the Federation . . ."—shall be amended as follows:

"1. Each Assembly shall elect twenty-two persons who with the President shall constitute the Executive Committee of the Federation."

The remainder of Article VIII remains unchanged.

Received as information.

c) The Business Committee recommends a change in the time schedule and a moving forward of election procedure in the assembly schedule. This was adopted.

(25) Tribute to the late Dr. Daniel T. Niles

The following resolution was submitted by the Resolutions Committee (cf. item 17):

The Fifth Assembly of the LWF has received with deep sorrow the news of the death of the Reverend Dr. Daniel T. Niles of Ceylon. This gifted leader, whom God raised up in his church made lasting and significant contributions in ecumenical progress in many ways. He was one of the most charismatic spiritual churchmen of modern times.

An eloquent preacher, a creative writer, and a man of profound insight, he fulfilled his ministry in the context of a deep personal devotion to Jesus Christ and pursued unwaveringly the course of bearing witness to the gospel. He was exceptional in his mastery of the thought forms of both eastern and western cultures, so that he could further communication between Christians whose approach to the gospel was conditioned by their respective traditions. With Christians throughout the world, we mourn his passing and thank God for his life and his faithful labors.

This was adopted.

The President reported that Professor Rajaratnam (India), and Dr. Nababan (Indonesia) would represent the Assembly at the memorial service for Dr. Niles to be held July 21 at the Ecumenical Center in Geneva.

(26) Greetings from the Rumanian Orthodox Church

Archimandrite Nestor Vornicescu presented greetings in the name of His Holiness, Patriarch Justinian of the Rumanian Orthodox Church.

Plenary VII
Tuesday morning and afternoon
July 21, 1970

(27) Greetings from Nonmember Churches

Greetings were brought by:

a) The Rev. Dr. Jacob A. O. Preuss, President of the Lutheran Church– Missouri Synod.

b) Superintendent Erich W. Eisenbeiss, representing the Evangelical Church in the Rhineland.

(28) Further Greetings

a) The General Secretary read a telegram from the Christian Peace Conference signed by Metropolitan Nikodim of Leningrad and Novgorod, Chairman of the Continuation Committee, and Janos Makowski, Acting General Secretary.

b) Pastor Papillon, pastor of the local congregation of the Reformed Church of France.

c) The President referred to a letter which was received from the Salvation Army regretting that no one had been able to be sent to the Assembly in Evian since the site had been changed.

(29) Amendment of Article VIII of the Constitution

The Business Committee submitted a proposal for amending the Constitution (see item 24b). The amendment would not, however, take effect immediately, but only one year from this date.

It was adopted, with only a few contrary votes.

(30) Report of the Nominations Committee

Bishop Wantula (Poland), chairman, reported that the Nominations Committee had held an open hearing. Candidates had been chosen not only from lists of the national committees, but also from delegations and individuals.

A question was raised concerning why, despite the request of the Open Hearing, the Nominations Committee had not presented in all instances more than one candidate for each position on the Executive Committee. In reply, Bishop Wantula stated that the Committee did take the suggestion of the Open Hearing into account, but could not, for various reasons, provide in all instances two names for each place. The mandate of the Nominations Committee did not derive from the Open Hearing but from the Assembly itself.

The Report of the Nominations Committee was accepted as follows:

For President

Fridtjov BIRKELI, b. 1906, Church of Norway
Mikko JUVA, b. 1918, Finnish Evangelical Church

For Executive Committee

1. *Africa* (2 to be elected plus 1 provisionally—cf. items 24b and 29)

Rakoto ANDRIANARIJAONA, b. 1918, Lutheran Church of Madagascar
Ezra GEBREMEDHIN, b. 1936, Mekane Yesus Church, Ethiopia
Judah KIWOVELE, b. 1927, Evangelical Lutheran Church in Tanzania
Daniel RAPOO, b. 1919, Evangelical Lutheran Church in Southern Africa

2. *Asia* (2 to be elected plus 1 provisionally)

Yoshiro ISHIDA, b. 1926, Evangelical Lutheran Church in Japan
Soritua A. E. NABABAN, b. 1933, Batak Protestant Christian Church, Indonesia
Kunchala RAJARATNAM, b. 1921, South Andhra Lutheran Church, India

3. *European Minority Churches—East* (1 to be elected)

Jan MICHALKO, b. 1912, Slovak Evangelical Church of the Augsburg Confession, Czechoslovakia

4. *Northern Europe* (1 each to be elected from Norway, Sweden, Finland, Denmark)

Fridtjov BIRKELI, b. 1906, Church of Norway
Ruben JOSEFSON, b. 1907, Church of Sweden
Mikko JUVA, b. 1918, Finnish Evangelical Church
Bodil SØLLING, b. 1922, Church of Denmark

5. *European Minority Churches—West* (1 to be elected)

Wilhelm DANTINE, b. 1911, Evangelical Church of the Augsburg Confession in Austria
Cord Hendrik LINDYER, b. 1917, Evangelical Lutheran Church in the Netherlands

6. *German Churches*

a) Federal Republic of Germany (3 to be elected)

Axel von CAMPENHAUSEN, Evangelical Lutheran Church in Bavaria
Hermann DIETZFELBINGER, b. 1908, Evangelical Lutheran Church in Bavaria
Horst GOLDNER, b. 1924, Evangelical Lutheran Church of Lübeck
Friedrich HÜBNER, b. 1911, Evangelical Lutheran Church of Schleswig-Holstein
Kurt SCHMIDT-CLAUSEN, b. 1920, Evangelical Lutheran Church of Hanover
Rudolf WEEBER, b. 1906, Evangelical Church of Württemberg

b) German Democratic Republic (2 to be elected)

Ingo BRAECKLEIN, b. 1906, Evangelical Lutheran Church in Thuringia
Ulrich von BRÜCK, b. 1914, Evangelical Lutheran Church of Saxony

7. *North America*

a) American Lutheran Church (2 to be elected)

Luvern RIEKE, b. 1922, Seattle, Washington
Fredrik A. SCHIOTZ, b. 1901, Minneapolis, Minnesota

b) Lutheran Church in America (2 to be elected)

Robert P. HETICO, b. 1925, Springfield, Ohio
Robert J. MARSHALL, b. 1918, New York, N.Y.

8. *South America* (1 to be elected and 1 provisionally)

Juan COBRDA, b. 1930, United Evangelical Lutheran Church—Argentina
Karl GOTTSCHALD, b. 1916, Evangelical Church of Lutheran Confession in Brazil

Additional nominations were made from the floor as follows:

Nominations for President

No further nominations were made. The President declared the nominations closed.

Nominations for the Executive Committee

1. *Africa*

Roland J. PAYNE, b. 1920, Lutheran Church of Liberia

2. *Asia*

Andrew HSIAO, b. 1926, Evangelical Lutheran Church of Hong Kong
Tunggul SIHOMBING, b. 1915, Batak Protestant Christian Church, Indonesia

3. *European Minority Churches—East*

Juro STRUHARIK, b. 1908, Slovak Evangelical Christian Church of the Augsburg Confession in Yugoslavia
Though nominated, Bishop Zoltan KALDY (Hungary) requested his name be withdrawn. His request was granted by the Assembly.

4. *Northern Europe*

Per VOKSØ, b. 1923, Church of Norway
Though nominated the Rev. Gunnar STÅLSETT (Norway) requested that his name be withdrawn. His request was granted by the Assembly.

5. *European Minority Churches—West*

Christian KEMPF, b. 1947, Church of the Augsburg Confession of Alsace and Lorraine
Though nominated, the Rev. Marc LIENHARD (France) requested that his name be withdrawn. His requested was granted by the Assembly.

6. *German Churches*

139

a) Federal Republic of Germany

Reinhard J.H.E. PIOCH, b. 1931, Evangelical Lutheran Church in the State of Hamburg
Hermann RINGELING, b. 1928, Evangelical Lutheran Church in the State of Hamburg

b) German Democratic Republic

Johannes CIESLAK, b. 1914, Evangelical Lutheran Church of Saxony
Traugott OHSE, b. 1928, Evangelical Lutheran Church of Mecklenburg
Joachim WIEBERING, b. 1934, Evangelical Lutheran Church of Mecklenburg

7. *North America*

a) American Lutheran Church

William HORDERN, Saskatoon, Canada
Walter TARPLEY, b. 1925, Columbus, Ohio

b) Lutheran Church in America

John WAGNER, Jr., b. 1929, Los Angeles, California

The President ruled that Mr. Tarpley should be paired on the ballot with Mr. Luvern Rieke since they were both laymen of the ALC and that Pastor Wagner be paired with Pastor Hetico since they were both pastors of the LCA. He also ruled that Dr. Hordern should be paired with himself, since the ELCC was a sister church of the ALC. This was challenged from the floor, but the ruling was upheld by a large majority.

8. *South America*

Gustavo RODRIGUEZ, Evangelical Lutheran Church, Colombia Synod

The nominations were declared closed.

A proposal was made from the floor that, in future elections for the Executive Committee, nominations be made not by the various National Committees but by a caucus of the delegates to the Assembly. The following proposal was also submitted:

Whereas: The LWF needs representation on the Executive Committee from various areas and churches, and

Whereas: These are best elected by the regions or churches they are to represent

Moved: That the appropriate committee of the LWF presents a plan for the election of the Executive Committee by region or by the church group selected for representation.

The President, with the consent of the Assembly, referred these two proposals to the new Executive Committee.

(31) Report of the Treasurer

The Treasurer, Dr. Rudolf Weeber (FRG), called attention to the fact that in 1969 approximately 44% of the amount raised in membership contributions came from the Lutheran churches of the United States and Canada, 50% from Germany and Scandinavia and 6% from the rest of the world. In comparison to the membership figures, the contribution from North America was extraordinarily high and in his opinion counterbalances the fact that other countries assume a larger share of responsibility for specific LWF programs. The time had come for setting priorities within the total scope of the present budget. He pointed out the strong support which had come from the churches for the work of World Service, World Mission, and Latin America, but underlined the need for the same support for the new Commission on Studies.

(32) Tribute to Representatives of Press, Radio, and Television (see item 66, no. 6).

Plenaries VIII and IX
Wednesday morning, afternoon and evening
July 22, 1970

(33) Report of the Policy and Reference Committee—Part I

In the material coming to PRC there were two kinds of recommendations:

a) Specific Recommendations regarding the Work of the LWF.

The report of the Executive Committee was received as information. As to the recommendations to the new Executive Committee which it contained, it was pointed out that they had been transmitted by the old Executive Committee to the new, and that they were transmitted without prejudice.

The recommendations, as amended, of the PRC with respect to the recommendations of the Commissions and Committees of the LWF were adopted by the Assembly.

Dr. Ahti Auranen (Finland) made a statement for inclusion in the minutes regarding LWF staffing procedures.

b) Section Reports and Recommendations

On recommendation of the PRC, the Assembly voted to receive the reports of the Sections.

The Recommendations of the PRC regarding the recommendations from Section I, Section II and Section III, as amended, were adopted by the Assembly. (See the Section Reports pp. 66 ff, 71 ff, and 83 ff.)

Section I

Dr. W. Ullrich (FRG) requested permission to record additional material from Section I since the report of Section I does not reflect that which came to expression in the discussions in Subsection 1.

Section II

A motion was made and seconded, in connection with the discussion of the recommendations of Section II, to adopt the Executive Committee's statement on Union Negotiations.

The statement was adopted as follows:

Statement concerning the Attitude of the LWF to Churches in Union Negotiations

When a member church of the LWF decides to enter union discussions with one or more non-Lutheran churches it may request advice and counsel from the LWF, which shall use the following guidelines in making a response:

a) Consistent with respect for both the fellowship and autonomy of member churches, the LWF will not attempt to prevent them from participating in union discussions but will rather assist them upon request.

b) A union of churches must be seen as a proper expression of the unity of the church when uniting churches have agreed upon a confessional statement of faith that witnesses to a right understanding of the gospel to serve as a guide for preaching and the administration of the sacraments. Becoming a part of a united church by a member church should not lead to a break in relationships with the LWF if the united church's confessional statement is in substantial agreement with the doctrinal basis of the LWF. Since united churches differ in nature, however, the LWF must find its appropriate relationships to such churches on an individual basis.

c) United churches which have or have had Lutheran constituencies, but which do not become members of the LWF, may be invited to send official visitors to LWF assemblies. Representatives of these churches may also take part in commissions, national committees, and other meetings under LWF sponsorship as consultants, or under certain circumstances as full members of commissions (Executive Committee minutes, 1965, p. 2).

d) Since a united church will discover its full integrity only after union is complete, all concerned parties should recognize that the church might well prefer not to maintain relationship with any organization representing a confessional family of faith. At the same time it should be recognized that a united church may desire a relationship with more than one confessional family. The LWF is willing to appoint representatives to discuss interchurch relationships with representatives from uniting churches and from the organizations of their families of faith.

e) The LWF has the conviction and desire that when member churches which have received aid from sister churches in the past unite with churches not of the Lutheran family, the donor churches should continue such financial support as will benefit the receiving church. The LWF will act in the same way.

Section III

On the recommendation of the PRC, two statements on world problems contained in the recommendations from Section III, Subsection 3 (a declaration on Racial Issues and Minority Problems and the Human Rights Declaration) were specifically referred to the Resolutions Committee.

Part I of the recommendation of Section III, Subsection 4 (Servanthood and Peace) was also referred to the Resolutions Committee.

Archbishop Josefson (Sweden) submitted a resolution which was in turn sent to the Resolutions Committee (the substance of this resolution was subsequently included in The Resolution on Human Rights—see item 44, no. 2).

(34) Name of the new Commission on Church Cooperation

This issue arose through the first report of the PRC. The Commission on World Mission at its meeting in St. Louis, with the support of the area consultations on Indonesia and India, had recommended to the Executive Committee at Evian that the name of the new Commission on Church Cooperation be changed to "Commission on Church Cooperation in World Mission". This was supported by a resolution adopted by Section I.

The PRC reported that this proposal did not have the support of the majority of PRC members, since "the proposed new name would cause problems in some areas of the work of this Commission".

A general debate ensued in which the following points were made:

a) The Assembly was meeting under the theme "Sent into the World" and that mission belongs to the essence of the church, some felt that the deletion of the word "mission" was a betrayal of the theme. Precisely because mission is under criticism, it is necessary to retain it in a comprehensive sense. Concern was expressed regarding the place of mission in the LWF. Mission implies more than cooperation, it means proclamation, and therefore the word "mission" is necessary.

b) In support of the name "Church Cooperation," others pointed out that the word "mission" was ambiguous and had negative connotations. There was a historical connection between mission and colonialism. Further misunderstanding arose in regard to mission as a function of the western churches, the "mission status" of the younger churches, as well as the connotation of proselytism. The constitution of the LWF and the terms of reference of the Commissions clearly pointed to mission as a task of the church. Mission, however, is not a function of the LWF, but a function of the churches. The LWF assists the churches to cooperate in their mission. From the point of view of the minority churches it might make ecumenical cooperation with other churches more difficult in some areas.

c) Various compromise suggestions were made.

The following titles were voted upon:
1. Commission on Church Cooperation
2. Commission on Church Cooperation and Evangelism
3. Commission on Church Cooperation and World Mission

The Assembly voted 115 to 58 to retain the name "Commission on Church Cooperation."

(35) Third Report of the Minutes Committee

With reference to item 25, the following additional information should be noted: Bishop Lilje (FRG), one of the Presidents of the WCC, was asked to join the delegation for the memorial service for Dr. Niles, and he agreed to do so.

The minutes were approved as distributed.

(36) Notice of Amendment to Article XIII of the Constitution

The Business Committee served notice of an amendment to the Constitution as follows:

"Alternative amendments may be made at a regularly called meeting of the Executive Committee by a unanimous vote of those present and voting or by a ¾ vote of the total membership, whichever is smaller."

This would provide an addition to Article XIII, Amendments, and would come before the Assembly tomorrow, July 23 (cf. items 46 and 59).

(37) Elections

The result of the election for President was: Mikko JUVA (148), Fridtjov BIRKELI (59). Professor Juva was declared to be elected president.

Prior to the election of the Executive Committee, it was made known that candidates J. STRUHARIK (Yugoslavia), T. OHSE (GDR), J. WIEBER- ING (GDR), and J. CIESLAK (GDR) declared themselves unwilling to serve if elected.

(38) Report of the Resolutions Committee

a) A statement prepared by Bishop Hans-Otto Wölber (FRG) was read (cf. item 23a).

Bishop Wölber indicated that he was not interested in the distribution of the statement as one coming from him personally, but rather that it expressed the mind of the Assembly (for discussion cf. items 48 and 55).

b) Following discussion, item 4 of the Section III, Subsection 3 statement on Human Rights was amended by the substitution of the parallel word- ing found in the report of the Resolutions Committee (cf. item 44, no. 6 in Resolution on Human Rights).

It was decided that the text of Section III on Human Rights should be dealt with first.

Plenary X
Thursday morning
July 23, 1970

Dr. Marshall (USA) proposed a substitute resolution combining the text of Section III with portions of the text of the Resolutions Com- mittee. Debate was postponed (cf. item 44).

c) The Report of the Resolutions Committee on the nomination of Dom Helder Camara for the Nobel Peace Prize was presented (cf. items 7e and 7g6). The Assembly decided to debate first the wording of the resolution as submitted to the Resolutions Committee by Professor Wingren (Sweden) and a number of delegates and other participants. This statement was adopted by a vote of 105 to 55, and reads as follows:

The Fifth General Assembly of the Lutheran World Federation, meeting at Evian-les-Bains, France, July 14-24, 1970, supports the nomination of Archbishop Helder Camara for the Nobel Peace Prize, with the following motivation:

1. Dom Helder Camara stands as a symbol for those who have devoted their lives to the struggle against oppression and inhuman conditions of life.

2. Camara has identified himself with those for whom he struggles. His work has concentrated on the slum areas, and both in Rio de Janeiro and Recife he has chosen to live without the abundance and many of the privileges that his position entitles him to. "He has", as he himself says, "become the voice of the voiceless".

3. After 1966 and Vatican II he has increasingly stressed interdependence between rich and poor nations. The need for change affects us all. Today's world gives all advantages, economical, political, social, and cultural, to the already highly developed nations. His goal has become the creation of a worldwide movement to alert the public to injustices and to engage the public in economic and political structural changes, which are necessary for a more righteous and human world.

4. Dom Helder Camara sees the way of nonviolence as the only possible one in Latin America, if bloodshed is to be avoided.

He sees the power of truth, justice, and love as the supreme force, also in today's world.

(39) Report of the Elections Committee on the Election of the new Executive Committee.

The following persons were declared elected on the first ballot:

Rakoto ANDRIANARIJOANA, Fridtjov BIRKELI, Ingo BRAECKLEIN, Ulrich von BRÜCK, Juan COBRDA, Hermann DIETZFELBINGER, Robert Paul HETICO, Ruben JOSEFSON, Judah KIWOVELE, Robert J. MARSHALL, Jan MICHALKO, Soritua A.E. NABABAN, Kunchala RAJARATNAM, Luvern RIEKE, Fredrik A. SCHIOTZ, Kurt SCHMIDT-CLAUSEN, Bodil SØLLING, Rudolf WEEBER; Elected previsionally (cf. items 24b and 29): Ezra GEBREMEDHIN, Karl GOTTSCHALD, Yoshiro ISHIDA.

As there was no absolute majority for any of the three candidates from the European Minority Churches/West, a second ballot was cast. Christian KEMPF was elected.

(40) Report on the Meeting of the Observer-Consultants

On behalf of the Observer-Consultants, Bishop Russell of the Anglican Communion reported briefly some of the comments made at their luncheon meeting. He made special reference to the openness and friendliness he met at this Assembly. The Open Hearings had been highlights which had provided an excellent opportunity to discuss the various aspects of the work of the LWF and the churches.

(41) Acknowledgment of Greetings

Greetings were acknowledged from

a) the Malagasy Protestant Church in France
b) the World Union of Catholic Women.

Plenary XI
Thursday afternoon and evening
July 23, 1970

(42) Fourth Report of the Minutes Committee

After minor corrections, the minutes were approved as presented.

(43) Greetings from a Representative of the World Methodist Council

Dr. Ole E. Borgen (Norway) brought greetings.

(44) Resolution on Human Rights

Dr. Marshall (USA) presented a document entitled "Resolution on Human Rights." Further amendments were referred to Dr. Marshall who accepted them for inclusion.

A motion was made and seconded to include a passage of the Resolutions Committee report in the statement. This was defeated.

A motion was made and seconded to delete all references to Brazil in the document. This was defeated.

The statement itself was adopted as follows:

Resolution on Human Rights

We are met in the Fifth Assembly of the LWF at Evian. We have gathered as a world family of Christians of the Lutheran confession and yet we are troubled. We all feel a strong concern for the wrongs which threaten and beset mankind, but are divided about the right course to follow in dealing with them.

We face a dilemma: either relevant statements must be couched in such general terms that they might be considered as exercises in pious rhetoric, or else very many issues or specific instances of violations of human worth would have to be dealt with individually on the basis of carefully documented research for which we seldom have the time or the technical resources.

One thing is clear: no one of us has the right to permit himself to be estranged from his brother by pointing the finger of blame exclusively at him. The hands of oppression in any country receive their support from many sources, so the blame must be shared by virtually all of us.

The Fifth Assembly, facing these difficulties, nevertheless cannot remain silent. As representatives of Lutheran churches, we still must believe that the conscience of Christians can be awakened to appropriate and constructive action.

The word "Brazil" is written indelibly in the minds of delegates to the Fifth Assembly of the Lutheran World Federation. Challenged by the theme "Sent into the World", it is a fact that much of the preparation applied this theme symbolically to the South American nations.

The section of the Assembly dealing with "Responsible Participation in Today's Society", and particularly that portion which relates to "Human Rights and Economic Justice", could not overlook the fact that there are dramatic and evident violations of human rights in the nation we once anticipated as the site of this Assembly.

Yet Brazil is not the only issue. Our concern is far more broad, reaching into an almost universal crisis symbolized by increasing violation of human rights. Brazil is simply a demonstration of a circumstance which exists in many other countries. The concern of this Assembly is directed to the deprivation of God-given human rights wherever, whenever, and for whatever reason it may occur.

The LWF Fifth Assembly is deeply aware of the deprivation of human justice that engulfs millions of people and renders them virtually helpless to assist themselves. It recognizes the manifestation of such deprivation in the violent acts of socio-political conditions in a number of countries, even to the extent of the suppression of political rights, imprisonment, and torture.

Further it is deplored that human rights are also deprived by less violent operations of unjust social and economic systems, in some instances by exploitation by rich land owners, in other instances by the manipulations of major industrial developments often controlled by residents of other countries. It is evident that victims of such activities are plunged into hunger, misery, and hopelessness.

The Fifth Assembly of the LWF pledges that, since the inescapable cost of personal discipleship in all such efforts is high, and aware of the great disparity between sensitivities in such matters generated at world assemblies and those prevalent at congregational levels, the delegates of this Fifth Assembly of the LWF will strive to their utmost, personally to arouse in their respective member churches a sense of desperate urgency for corrective action in the areas of social justice, human rights, and world peace.

In the face of these circumstances and seeking to be obedient to the Lord and Savior Jesus Christ as he is known through the Scriptures, be it resolved by the Assembly that:

1. The delegates declare their judgment that it is appropriate and necessary for Christian churches to scrutinize such conditions in their respective national situations and to help to prepare their members for corrective actions at individual and corporate levels through available religious and secular instrumentalities and channels.

2. The member churches and recognized congregations be requested to report to the General Secretary if possible not later than July 1, 1971 about actions taken and immediate plans regarding the issues. This report should, if possible, include the following aspects:

   a) The church's understanding of its social and political responsibility in its specific situation.

   b) Steps considered for concrete implementation.

   c) Suggestions how sister churches could provide help.

3. The churches be urged to provide ways, means, and incentive for a study by their respective memberships of the Universal Declaration of Human Rights and the applicability of this declaration to the circumstances within the nation of such member church.

4. Special study be given to the articles of the Declaration which are most evidently being violated in this day: namely Article 2 on life, freedom and security; Article 6 on torture and punishment; Article 9 on imprisonment and exile; Article 10 on right to a fair trial; Article 18 on freedom of thought, conscience and religion; Article 19 on free expression of thought and comment; and Article 26 on education.

5. The churches be urged to give special attention to the desirability of expanding this declaration, either through interpretation or amendment, to emphasize the rights of groups of people and social orders, in addition to the freedoms assured to the individual.

6. The appropriate agencies of the LWF be urged to increasingly respond to the needs of those who are imprisoned and their families, and others who are persecuted for conscience's sake and those who require humanitarian or social assistance in consequence of their struggle against oppression. Such assistance may include scholarships to exiles, social and development services in areas liberated from colonial rule, legal aid and representation and cooperation with organizations which specialize in such activities.

7. The Executive Committee be instructed to involve the LWF in more intensive studies on the international level of these problems, preferably in cooperation with the WCC, other world confessional bodies, and specialized secular agencies, submitting relevant data periodically to the member churches.

Mr. Gustavo Rodriguez, Colombia, read the following statement:

"The delegations from Argentina and Colombia want to register in the minutes the fact that we oppose the pointing out of a Latin American country, namely, Brazil, as a symbol of the violation of human rights and economic injustice. The Assembly knows that these violations occur in several countries of the world. As a part of the pressure of developed countries we accept this declaration. Do we have a choice? It has been approved by the industrialized countries who are worried about the violation of our human rights."

Pastor Helmut Frenz, Chile, made the motion that

"A special commission composed of three persons be nominated in order to present to the Brazilian government the concerns of the LWF as contained in the Resolution on Human Rights which had been adopted."

This was approved.

(45) Words of Gratitude to the Assembly Staff

The General Secretary presented some of the key persons who had been working on the Assembly preparations and operations: Rev. Carl H. Mau Jr., Miss Vera Henrich, Mr. Hans-Andreas Krogmann, Mr. Claus Dölling, Rev. Christian Krause. Gratitude was also expressed to the many others—staff, volunteers, etc.—who had worked with them.

(46) Amendment to Article XIII of the Constitution (continued)

The President recalled that announcement had been made of intent to amend the Constitution (cf. item 36).

The fear was expressed that the door should not be opened to indiscriminate amendment of the Constitution, and that the full power of the churches to amend the constitution not be jeopardized. Alternate wordings were referred back to be consolidated into one proposal (cf. item 59).

(47) Report of the Ad Hoc Committee of the Assembly on the Response to the Visit of Cardinal Willebrands.

Professor Knutson read the report of the ad hoc committee. Objections were voiced by delegates from a number of areas, pointing out that the international dialog with the Roman Catholic Church had caused confusion in the congregations, since renewal in the Catholic Church and dialog possibilities did not everywhere exist to the same degree.

Action was postponed to make the inclusion of amendments possible.

The following recommendation was adopted:

It is recommended that the dialog between the Lutheran World Federation and the Roman Catholic Church be continued in an appropriate form even after the completion of the work of the present and projected Study Commissions.

(48) Discussion of the Statement prepared by Bishop Wölber

Bishop Wölber introduced the statement (cf. items 23a and 38a) emphasizing that the attitude of man and not just the conditions in which he lives must be changed. Here the work of the Holy Spirit had to be emphasized. In pointing to the responsibility of man, one must point to him to whom man is responsible. The personality of God must therefore be brought out clearly. "Sent into the World" makes it necessary to note the difference between the church and the world and raises the issue of maintaining the identity of the church. As we learn to see the political implications of the work of the church, we should not lose sight of the fact that to the church is given the task of proclaiming an ultimate word of redemption.

After considerable debate, a motion was made and seconded to refer the matter to a small ad hoc committee to bring in suggested amendments. The proposal was narrowly defeated.

Final disposal of the document was deferred (cf. item 55).

(49) Greetings from the Lutheran Church of Australia.

President F. Max Lohe brought greetings on behalf of his church.

Plenaries XII and XIII
Friday morning and afternoon
July 24, 1970

(50) Fifth Report of the Minutes Committee

The minutes were approved as corrected.

The President explained that the minutes of the remaining Plenaries would be submitted for approval to the new Executive Committee.

(51) Final Report of the Credentials Committee

Dr. Payne (Liberia), presented the final report of this committee:

The following are totals for those registered and accredited at this Assembly:

Delegates—from Africa	30
—from Asia	30
—from Europe	113
—from North America	32
—from Latin America	11
TOTAL number of Delegates	216

Official Visitors	33
Advisers	112
Observer-Consultants	19
Staff—International	49
Coopted Press	27
Accredited Press	119
TOTAL number of Participants thus far registered	575

The report was accepted.

(52) Report of the Policy and Reference Committee—Part II

a) Reports and Recommendations from the Open Hearings

1. A question was raised concerning several recommendations from the Open Hearing on Education which did not appear in the report. Dr. Rieke (USA) auditor of the PRC in this Open Hearing, gave the assurance that these would be brought to the attention of the Executive Committee.

2. With regard to the Open Hearing on World Mission, a question was raised as to why the report of the Committee on the Church and the Jews had not been placed before the Assembly, since the report requested the Assembly to approve it. In response it was stated that the report had been submitted to the Executive Committee which had referred it to the Open Hearing of World Mission. The concerns of this committee were to be referred to the new Commission on Studies.

On recommendation of the PRC the Assembly voted to refer all the reports from the Open Hearings of the Commissions to the new Executive Committee for information.

b) Additional Recommendations from Delegates

Three additional recommendations were made. Two were referred to the new Executive Committee and the third concerning the dissemination of study material from the Hungarian, Slovakian, and Swedish churches was referred to the General Secretariat.

(53) Statement on the LWF'S Role in World Mission

Rev. Gunnar Stålsett (Norway) read a statement which had been mimeographed and distributed to the participants. The statement was unanimously adopted as follows:

Whereas the role of the LWF in the field of world mission has been discussed in this general Assembly, and whereas this Assembly has sanctioned to omit the word mission in the name of the Commission now taking over the responsibility hitherto carried on by CWM, and whereas strong concerns have been expressed that the LWF's role in the task of world mission be clarified, the Assembly calls the attention of member churches especially to the report of Section I at this Assembly dealing with our obligation in mission and the power of the gospel in mission, where it is stated:

"We believe that just as Jesus Christ was sent by God into the world to redeem the world, so we have been sent by Jesus joyfully to proclaim the gospel in love and with justice. (3)

The power of the gospel is evident to us when we both individually and as a church are confronted with our own sin, impossible to repair; in our confrontation with our own death, impossible to avoid; and in our confrontation with the total need of mankind, impossible to neglect. (5)

Jesus Christ who himself is the gospel, has descended to our anguish. To accept the fact that I am a sinner, and that I, in spite of that, receive a new life and am called to a new service, is to have forgiveness of sins through the cross of Christ. To accept the fact that death is at the door before us, but that we, in spite of this fact, go from life to life, is to receive the resurrection of the dead through the resurrection of Christ. Through this same gospel we are set free to fulfill the will of God. To accept the fact that the needs of our neighbors direct our deeds and actions in our service to the Lord, obligates us to a constant review of our ministry to the world. The service which we thereby receive from Christ as members of his body, gives us the power to fulfill this ministry, even in an hostile environment. (6) In these confrontations the Holy Spirit also today through the gospel gives us power to live and serve and celebrate. This power we cannot receive without being sent to the world, and in our going out to witness and serve we are receiving this power according to our needs." (7)

According to this conviction the Lutheran World Federation urges its member churches and related agencies faithfully to work for the proclamation of the gospel to all nations.

We furthermore call attention to the terms of reference for the Commission on Church Cooperation where it expresses that it on its part will continue to support Lutheran churches and groups as they endeavor to carry out the mission imperative of the Lord. It will continue to facilitate contacts and exchange of resources, information, counsel, in such a way as to strengthen the life and witness of related churches in all parts of the world. It will provide programs requested by member churches where it is not feasible for the churches to conduct programs themselves. In this endeavor it will also continue to provide for meetings of churches, mission societies, and related organizations on a global or regional basis as necessary.

(54) Proposed Resolution on the LWF'S Attitude toward Apartheid in the Churches.

The PRC Report, Part II contained a resolution regarding the stance of

153

the LWF in regard to the fact that churches in South Africa apparently elected "to live under principles of apartheid." The PRC submitted the following recommendation:

a) The Assembly approve the principles:

1. Lutheran church black and white members should be willing at all times to commune together.

2. The principles and practices of apartheid should be opposed.

3. LWF should not grant funds to churches which do not accept principles 1 and 2.

4. LWF funds to be channeled into those nonwhite African churches in an effort to provide the economic and spiritual support that they so desperately need in their quest for equal justice.

b) The Assembly recommend to the Executive Committee:

A delegation be sent from the LWF to Lutheran churches in the Republic of South Africa to urge them to bring their racial practices into conformity with the principles of Christian fellowship as rapidly as possible and that the delegation report its findings to the Executive Committee and that the Executive Committee submit to member churches a report concerning its subsequent deliberations and any further action which it believes appropriate.

In the course of debate, the Rev. Müller-Nedebock (ELC in Southern Africa, Hermannsburg) made a statement (included in Unabridged Minutes) in which he like others from various churches in South Africa pointed out that official pulpit and altar fellowship already existed between the Lutheran Churches in South Africa and that slow but steady progress was being made for Lutheran unity. Action such as proposed by the PRC might endanger such progress.

The resolution with a number of suggested amendments was referred back to the PRC for consideration (cf. item 60).

(55) Theological Statement

The President called upon Dr. Edgar Carlson (USA) who had agreed with Bishop Wölber (FRG) on amendments to the statement of Bishop Wölber (see items 23a, 38a and 48). The amendments were adopted.

The Assembly voted to transmit this statement together with the lecture

154

of Professor Tödt to the member churches and commend it to them for study and reactions:

Special Theological Statement

1) Having voiced our depression as well as our responsibility in light of the injustice and absence of freedom and peace in the world, we wish to speak clearly and unqualifiedly, not only of social problems, but of the individual's responsibility in society. In this connection, we wish to address ourselves not only to the individual's dependence on external structures, but also to the chaos within the structure of his own self. Back of all the perplexities lie not only, e.g., rapid and unmastered changes in the world or our inability to achieve better relations. Back of them lies also human greed, hunger for power and self-justification. Man makes himself the measure of all things. These preconditions of our nature we call sin. Thus, we must not only understand our world better—we must undergo a change. We not only need a new consciousness—we need a transformation of our nature and our will.

2) In our experience, man undergoes a fundamental change only when he gains a new relation to his origin and destiny. This fundamental change in relationships is what we have in mind when we speak of a relationship to God. We thus appeal to all to seek God anew, especially in him whom we know as Jesus Christ, to pray and listen to his Word.

3) We say this, not only because we are aware of all the external misery, but also because we see a psychic hunger everywhere, a hunger depicted in irritations, aggressiveness, flight toward intoxication, and in an ideologically based and illusionary yearning for a world without conflict. We say this, further, because the yearning for peace will not only be stilled with a new order of world peace, but only when man is ready to fill that new order with the spirit of peace. We say this, finally, because although justice is a very lofty earthly aim, man's dignity and right also consists in waiving his rights and, when his neighbor requires it, in sacrificing himself and in suffering. We are not thereby unmindful of how much irreparable suffering falls to man's lot, of how he fears his transitoriness or of the fact that in the end he must die.

4) Confronted with these present dangers, we cannot conceal the possibility that the solution might already have slipped from men's hands, that however we might fight against it, we must reckon with catastrophes of apocalyptic dimensions. All this leads us to witness to our fellow men that Christians believe in a total new creation, turning their gaze toward it in prayer and worship.

5) Confessing all this, we call mankind, shaken by crisis, not merely to

social responsibility, but to a life of faith and prayer. We are convinced that back of our misery there is that catastrophe in our relation to God, robbing us of all criteria for human existence and of any opportunity for a new spirit. But we see that the catastrophe can be overcome when man discovers that his relation to his origin and destiny is freed from all fear and anxiety by the unlimited love of God which has appeared in Jesus Christ. God accepts man simply because he is man. We should accept one another as well as ourselves. This "yes" to one another, this "yes" to ourselves is the origin of new relationships in human society.

(56) Statement on the Visit of Cardinal Willebrands

The statement with amendments introduced by Professor Kent Knutson (USA) was adopted by the Assembly:

The Fifth Assembly of the Lutheran World Federation gratefully acknowledges the presence of Jan Cardinal Willebrands and the Roman Catholic observers. It views the personal appearance of the President of the Secretariat for Promoting Christian Unity as a sign of growing understanding between Roman Catholic and Lutheran churches, as well as an encouragement to strive further toward that fellowship required by our churches for their common mission and service in the world.

At the same time, we see in the presence of Cardinal Willebrands more than a significant ecumenical gesture. We are grateful that in his plenary address he made the theme of our Assembly his own, and thus made a valuable contribution to our work.

We have paid particular attention to the cardinal's statements concerning the person and theology of Martin Luther. We are aware of the significance of the fact that on such a notable occasion, an eminent representative of the Roman Catholic Church should commit himself to a more equitable evaluation of the Reformer and the Reformation. We are convinced that this appropriation of the results of modern Catholic research on Luther and the Reformation represents a unique and important step toward a deeper and more far-reaching understanding between our churches. In accordance with the commandment of truth and love which should determine this understanding, differences still existing in the evaluation of the Reformation and tensions in church practice in various parts of the world should be openly acknowledged. The recognition of these differences does not inhibit understanding, but is the prerequisite for it; it does not prevent, but furthers it.

It is also in accordance with this commandment of truth and love that we as Lutheran Christians and congregations be prepared to acknowledge that the judgment of the Reformers upon the Roman Catholic Church and its theology was not entirely free of polemical distortions, which in part have been perpetuated to the present day.

We are truly sorry for the offense and misunderstanding which these polemic elements have caused our Roman Catholic brethren. We remember with gratitude the statement of Pope Paul VI to the Second Vatican Council in which he communicates his plea for forgiveness for any offense caused by the Roman

Catholic Church. As we together with all Christians pray for forgiveness in the prayer our Lord has taught us, let us strive for clear, honest, and charitable language in all our conversations.

Recommendation: (cf. item 47 for accompanying recommendations).

(57) Report of the Ad Hoc Committee on Lutheran/Reformed Conversations

Bishop Hübner (FRG), chairman of the Committee, presented the report. Rev. Mobbs, Observer-Consultant from the World Alliance of Reformed Churches, expressed his appreciation of the report, mentioning that it would be brought to the attention of the Assembly of the World Alliance of Reformed Churches, to be held in Nairobi in August.

The report described both the breadth and intensity of conversations between the two groups and gave a partial survey of the countries and areas where discussions have been or are being conducted. Because of the special historical and theological relationship between the Lutheran and Reformed churches, dialog must look toward full church fellowship. This must, however, always be seen in the wider context of the wholeness of the Christian church. The Committee agreed with the proposal that church fellowship between the Lutheran, Reformed and united churches of Europe should be implemented by way of a common declaration, suggested by the traditional model of a "concord".

The report noted with regret the difficulty of implementing the practical implications of a theological consensus. Various suggestions were made toward overcoming the hiatus between theological consensus and its practical realization within the church.

Both the World Alliance of Reformed Churches and the Lutheran World Federation have a particular role to play with respect to the life of the younger churches. The two world organizations should seek to encourage in new ways their respective member churches to enter into fellowship and common action and conversation, looking toward union where they have not already done so.

Regarding a closer relationship between these two world organizations, it recommended that: The Lutheran World Federation and the World Alliance of Reformed Churches work together when planning their assemblies; agreement be sought with regard to the foundation and care of overseas congregations; their mutual understanding of their ecumenical commitment and their role in the further development of the ecumenical movement be discussed; and, possibilities be sought for a closer working relationship in the field of theology.

The report was received and the following two recommendations were adopted:

1) That the report of the Assembly ad hoc committee concerning Lutheran/Reformed conversations be brought before the member churches of the LWF for careful study, including the documents and publications appended to it.

2) That in planning and executing future studies or consultations, the Study Commission of the LWF keep in mind and, wherever feasible, make use of the possibility for cooperative endeavor with the Theological Section of the WARC.

(58) Statement by Rev. Carl-Henric Grenholm (Sweden)

Rev. Grenholm requested and received permission to have a statement included in the minutes (cf. Unabridged Minutes) concerning the opinions he had expressed about Colombia at the Youth Evening of the Assembly.

(59) Amendment to Article XIII of the Constitution (continued)

After considerable discussion of the text (see items 36 and 46), and the advisability of adopting such an amendment, the Assembly voted to refer the proposed amendment to the new Executive Committee for further consideration and report to the next Assembly.

(60) Resolution on Communion of All Races

The chairman of the PRC reported a proposed revision of the resolution previously submitted (see item 54). Considerable debate ensued on the advisability of sending a delegation to South Africa. The opinion was expressed that a delegation could only be sent if invited by the churches. Others feared that the LWF was functioning in this matter as "a super church". The strong opinion, on the other hand, was expressed that this resolution should not be weakened further. Several amendments were adopted and others defeated. The following amended resolution was adopted.

a) The Assembly approves the principles:

1. In the Lutheran church members of all races should be willing at all times to receive communion together.

2. The Lutheran churches should oppose the principles and practices of racial discrimination and segregation.

b) The Assembly recommends to the Executive Committee that:

1. A delegation be sent from the LWF to churches where the above principles constitute a special problem to urge them to bring their racial practices into conformity with the principles of Christian fellowship as rapidly as possible and that the delegation report its findings to the Executive Committee and that the Executive Committee submit to member churches a report concerning its subsequent deliberations and any further action which it believes appropriate.

2. In order to encourage the quest for equal justice the two principles shall serve as criteria in providing assistance to churches.

(61) Resolution regarding Interim Procedures and Future LWF Assemblies

The Assembly voted to adopt the resolution as amended:

Resolution regarding Interim Procedures and Future LWF Assemblies

RESOLVED: 1) that, in order to establish procedures for more effective implementation of the work of the LWF and particularly the work of the Commissions in various regions as well as in the national committees and member churches, we urgently request the Executive Committee:

    a. to establish priorities in the work of the Commissions as well as to coordinate their respective responsibilities according to such guidelines as may be established by the Assembly;

    b. to encourage and facilitate working groups of expert and competent persons in the national committees and where possible also in the member churches which would be in a position to work together with the Commissions as partners in dialog and in the clarification of issues;

    c. to sponsor international consultations of the LWF at regional levels during the periods between the assemblies which would aim to evaluate the work of the Commissions for the churches in such regions;

    2) that since experience has shown that current procedures for conducting LWF general assemblies are not adequate to carry out its purposes, the Executive Committee is instructed to examine the structure and working arrangements for future assemblies in the light of the proposals of the present assembly and the experience of other ecumenical groups, and to report its findings to the member churches at the earliest opportunity. In this connection, relevant proposals made by delegates to this Assembly or subsequently by member churches shall be taken into consideration.

(62) Resolution regarding Guidelines for Assemblies

A resolution had been introduced (cf. item 7k) and referred to the PRC. The Assembly voted to adopt the resolution as presented.

Resolution regarding Guidelines for Assemblies

The Fifth Assembly, after hearing the report of the General Secretary about the developments leading up to the change of site for the Assembly, has at length discussed the reasons behind the decision and its implications for the Lutheran World Federation.

Without passing any judgment regarding the decision at the Officers' Meeting on May 20-21, 1970, and the many actions and statements by the LWF and member churches in Brazil and elsewhere that led up to the decisions, the Assembly

DEPLORES that the LWF, by changing the site of the Assembly has lost a great opportunity to get acquainted with and bear witness to a part of the world that increasingly must be the concern of both the Federation and all member churches;

RECOMMENDS that the Executive Committee, in its study of the role of LWF assemblies, develop clear guidelines for the division of responsibilities between the LWF and the host church.

(63) Statement on Servanthood and Peace

The Resolutions Committee submitted without prejudice both the statement of Section III, Subsection 4, "Servanthood and Peace" in its original wording and a proposed revision which deleted reference to specific countries.

The proposed revision of the Resolutions Committee, as amended in plenary, was adopted:

Statement on Servanthood and Peace

1. On the basis of their tradition, Lutheran churches are in danger of assuming distant neutrality toward the social problems of their countries. They should thus be encouraged to realize their mission in the world by unequivocally advancing the cause of those who suffer from unjust structures. In addition to private, personal action, congregations should make use of information and means furnished by competent institutions, e.g., by social agencies and scientific organizations. Such will require the needed alteration of church structures.

2. Since the 19th century, the national state has gathered its citizens' loyalty to itself and thus hindered a transnational orientation. An ecumenical reorientation of loyalties is required. To further the dissolution of military systems which threaten life through their worldwide security and juridical systems, congregations and churches, above all, should strengthen and support the United Nations Organizations

   a. In special resolutions,

   b. In establishing structures which, e.g., facilitate sanctions—at least in a moral fashion—against the superpowers, whenever these endanger the UN charter.

   c. In working to seat all states in the UN.

3. In a highly technological world, in which use of power creates ever greater dangers, opportunities for peaceful resistance for peaceful transformation of destructive conditions should be employed. The basic types are concrete action and planned development. The impulse of the Sermon on the Mount toward rejection of violence should thus be taken seriously and in a new way. This impulse is often taken with more intense seriousness by nonchristians than by Christians. For example, the proposal for the holding of a conference on European security would seem to offer hopeful possibilities, and churches in this area may find ways to encourage and assist in working toward its goals.

(64) Statement on Racial Issues and Minority Problems—A Challenge for the Church

The Resolutions Committee reported that it had considered the Report of Section III, Subsection 3, on Racial Issues and Minority Problems. The Resolutions Committee presented to the Assembly, without prejudice, a revised text as well as the original. After considerable debate the revised text with minor amendments was adopted.

Statement on Racial Issues and Minority Problems—A Challenge for the Church

The issue of minority and nationality group relations throughout the world is a major and urgent problem. Minority people in many parts of the world have been prevented from achieving their full potential as productive citizens by the attitudes of those in power and in the position of authority. Special outrage is expressed for the continuing forms of antisemitism which appear in many countries.

Racial tensions throughout the world have created problems of such magnitude as to demand the attention of the whole Christian community. We regret and condemn all forms of racism and racial discrimination and hereby recommend that the LWF and its member churches utilize their resources and energies in the development of programs which will help to eliminate all forms of discrimination both in church and society.

In an effort to further the cause of justice and prevent explosions, the church must accept the premise that its future efforts should be extended and expanded to overcome past injustices and move toward greater respect for the human rights and the dignity of people in all nations of the world, as they strive to attain:

1. full and equal employment opportunities;
2. law enforcement and justice administered with all of the protective safeguards inherent in proper administration;
3. housing that is safe, sanitary, and unrestricted in its availability;
4. improved health and welfare services that are delivered on an equitable basis as a basic right of the recipient;
5. educational reforms designed to provide better preparation for living as a productive member of the changing social order;
6. full opportunity for the expression of their religious faith;
7. equitable involvement in political, business, economic, and professional life.

We thereby endorse and support not only Christians but all men of good will throughout the world as they strive to eliminate racial discrimination and to achieve racial justice in society.

161

(65) Sympathy Resolutions

(what follows is a summary of the Resolutions adopted)

a) The Assembly noted with sorrow the sudden death of Professor Ulrich S. Leupold (Canada), who had assisted in preparing the new edition of *Laudamus*. A resolution of sympathy and appreciation was adopted.

b) Resolutions of tribute were addressed to the wives of three former LWF Executive Committee members who have been called from this life:

Mrs. Franklin Clark Fry
Mrs. Rajah B. Manikam
Mrs. Ernesto Schlieper

c) A message was addressed to Bishop Hermann Dietzfelbinger, a member of both the old and new Executive Committees, who for reasons of health was unable to attend the Assembly, wishing him complete recovery.

(66) Expressions of Gratitude

The Resolutions Committee presented the following resolutions which were adopted:

Expressions of Gratitude

I) The decision made at a very late date to move the Fifth Assembly of the LWF from Porto Alegre imposed upon the Lutheran World Federation staff an enormous load of work which could not have been carried out, had it not been for substantial help suddenly solicited and readily granted by many organizations and agencies. The Assembly expresses its deep appreciation to all those inside and outside the LWF who so willingly cooperated in this emergency to make it possible for the Assembly to carry out its functions at Evian.

The Assembly expresses it gratitude to those involved in major ways, as follows:

1. We express our thanks to the Alliance Nationale des Eglises Luthériennes en France (National Alliance of Lutheran Churches in France) which without hesitation accepted the responsibility of the role of host church;

2. We are also grateful to the French Protestant Council which welcomed the Assembly to the site in France;

3. The city authorities of Evian, and the Tourist Office, without the extraordinary efforts of which the successful completion of local arrangements would not have been possible, also merit and are hereby given our deep appreciation;

4. The Assembly acknowledges with particular gratitude the fraternal graciousness of Cardinal Marty, President of the Episcopal Conference (RC) of

France, of the Bishop of Annecy, Monseigneur Jean Sauvage and his associates, in making available the use of their facilities in Evian, specifically the Roman Catholic Parish Church (Notre Dame de Grace) for the purpose of worship services, and space at the schools of St. Bruno and St. Joseph, where meeting rooms and administrative offices of the Assembly have been located. This act of Christian cooperation is a tangible demonstration of the gratifying developments in our times which are expressive of the unity which we possess in our Lord Jesus Christ, and for which we praise him;

5. The Assembly notes with appreciation that the World Council of Churches and other organizations in the Ecumenical Center in Geneva readily placed at the disposal of the LWF considerable assistance through the services of personnel and equipment. For such emergency help in time of need, a special word of thanks is due them and is hereby heartily expressed;

6. The Assembly's thanks also are extended to the large number of persons coming from many lands who have served on a voluntary basis both prior to and during this Assembly. Their cheerful readiness to help in every possible way has won the gratitude of the participants, and their performance of innumerable details connected with the operation of the Assembly has been a significant contribution to the work of the LWF.

II) The Assembly records its indebtedness to the Assembly Preparatory Committee of the Evangelical Church of Lutheran Confession in Brazil, mentioning especially its Chairman, Karl Gottschald, and its Director, Guido Tornquist, for their arduous efforts exerted over a two year period, which were in a large measure nullified by the relocation of the Assembly. We assure them that their work merits our deep appreciation and that we share their disappointment, and that of the many pastors and congregations who had looked forward to our coming, that their arrangements so fully made were not carried through.

III) The Assembly has been greatly impressed by the services rendered by the several LWF units as recorded in the report covering the years 1963-1969. These accomplishments testify to the high degree of competency and dedication with which the staff members performed their assigned tasks.

Although the work of the General Secretary, of the Associate General Secretary, and the Department Directors merit special mention, the Assembly does not overlook the indispensable role of their colleagues associated in the worldwide activities of the LWF. The Assembly hereby commends them for the faithful performance of their duties.

IV) Since the Helsinki Assembly, the world has passed through seven years which have no parallel in human history. The necessity of facing complex situations and of making grave decisions has placed an extraordinary burden upon the Executive Committee and the Officers of the Federation, a fact which the Assembly acknowledges, together with its appreciation of their faithful performance of their responsibilities.

The Assembly furthermore thanks God for the capable leadership provided by its outgoing President, Dr. Fredrik A. Schiotz. It is evident that a churchman of his temperament, experience and insight was especially equipped to guide the LWF through this difficult period. President Schiotz has served the LWF well at a great personal price of time, energy, and dedication. His patience, his objectivity, his ability to effect communication in polarized situations, and his pastoral concern regarding the state of the member churches in general and the LWF in particular have endeared him to a multitude of persons, both within and without the Lutheran family. We thank God for raising up this leader to serve us and pray that he will grant President Schiotz abundant strength to serve his Lord and his church in many creative ways in the years to come.

V) We, the delegates of the Fifth Assembly of the LWF, in session at Evian-les-Bains, France, July 14-24, 1970, have listened with gladness to the greeting brought from the World Alliance of Reformed Churches by its President, Professor Wilhelm Niesel. We also have received with gratification reports regarding the fruitful progress thus far achieved in the course of consultations between representatives of our respective world confessional bodies, and anticipate that in the years ahead expanded opportunities for common study and work in areas of mutual concerns will develop.

Furthermore, we in the LWF extend to the World Alliance of Reformed Churches, meeting in Nairobi, Kenya, August 20-30, 1970, our fraternal good wishes accompanied by our prayers that God will bless your endeavors so that his will among men be furthered thereby and the healing and freeing power of his love may be released effectively wherever your witness to him is manifested.

(67) Proposal regarding Election Procedures

Professor Goppelt (FRG) proposed that the Executive Committee "define detailed election procedures in keeping with the structure of the Federation". This proposal to be recorded in the minutes for the attention of the new Executive Committee.

(68) Statement by the Churches in Exile

The representatives of the Lutheran Churches in Exile of Estonia, Latvia, and Lithuania requested that a statement which they would submit in writing not be read but be recorded in the minutes (protocol copy). The President requested the consent of the Assembly, which was granted.

(69) Personal Statement by OKR Heidler

Rev. Fritz Heidler (GDR) requested permission to make a personal statement concerning the conduct and working methods of the Assembly, this was granted (included in Unabridged Minutes).

(70) Installation of the new President and new Executive Committee

Dr. Fredrik A. Schiotz (USA) conducted the service of installation.

(71) Address of the new President, Professor Mikko Juva

Professor Mikko Juva (Finland), the new President, addressed the Assembly. His address was greeted with sustained applause.

(72) Vespers were conducted by the chaplains, the Rev. Ronald Swenson, Pastor of the English-speaking congregation of the Evangelical Lutheran Church in Geneva, and Dr. Friedrich-Wilhelm Künneth, Secretary of the Commission on Worship and Spiritual Life.

(73) On a motion by the delegates of the Lutheran Church in Kenya, which was seconded and adopted, the President declared the Assembly adjourned.